KICK-ASS

MARK MILLAR
WRITER AND CO-CREATOR

JOHN ROMITA JR.
PENCILLER AND CO-CREATOR

TOM PALMER
INKS

DEAN WHITE
COLOURS

CHRIS ELIOPOULOS
LETTERS

JOHN BARBER
ORIGINAL SERIES EDITOR

TITAN BOOKS

FOR ICON

MICHAEL HORWITZ
ASSISTANT EDITOR

JEFF YOUNGQUIST
SENIOR EDITOR, SPECIAL PROJECTS

ANTHONY DIAL & IRENE LEE
PRODUCTION

DAVID GABRIEL
SENIOR VICE PRESIDENT OF SALES

DAVID BOGART
SVP OF BUSINESS AFFAIRS & TALENT MANAGEMENT

JOE QUESADA
EDITOR IN CHIEF

DAN BUCKLEY
PUBLISHER

ALAN FINE
EXECUTIVE PRODUCER

KICK-ASS
ISBN: 9781848565357

Published by Titan Books
A division of Titan Publishing Group Ltd.
144 Southwark Street
London
SE1 0UP

Kick-Ass comic strip © 2010 Mark Millar and John S. Romita.

A CIP catalogue record for this title is available from the British Library.

First edition: March 2010.
10 9 8 7 6 5 4 3 2 1

Printed in Spain.

What did you think of this book? We love to hear from our
readers. Please email us at: readerfeedback@titanemail.com,
or write to us at the above address.

To receive advance information, news, competitions, and
exclusive Titan offers online, please register by clicking the
"sign up" button on our website: **www.titanbooks.com**

I always wondered why nobody did it before me.

I mean, all those comic book movies and television shows, you'd think at least *one* eccentric loner would have stitched himself a costume.

Is everyday life really so exciting?

Are schools and offices really so thrilling that I'm the only one who ever *fantasized* about this?

C'mon. Be honest with yourself.

We all planned to be a superhero at *some* point in our lives.

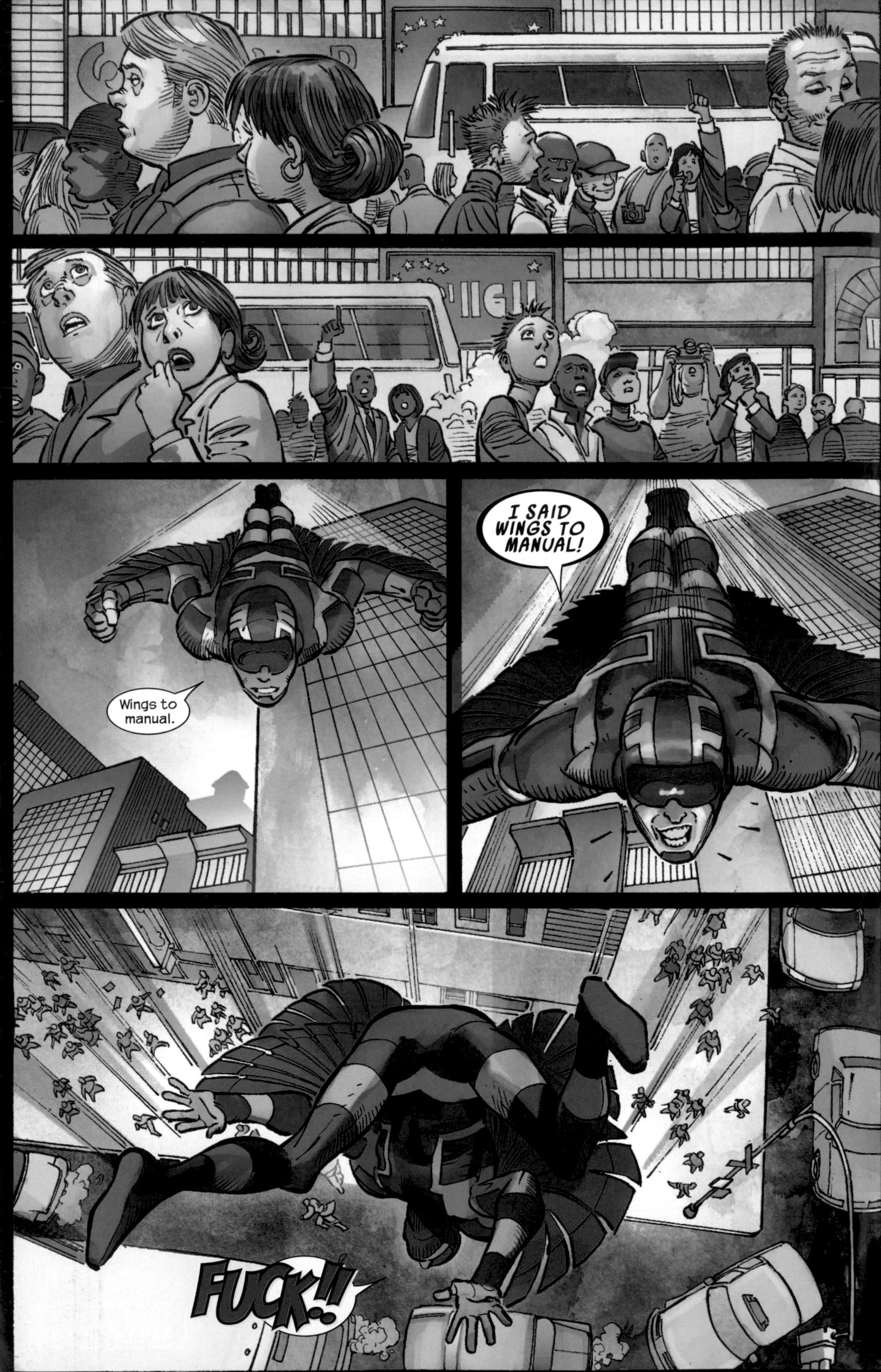

Wings to manual.
I SAID WINGS TO MANUAL!
FUCK!!

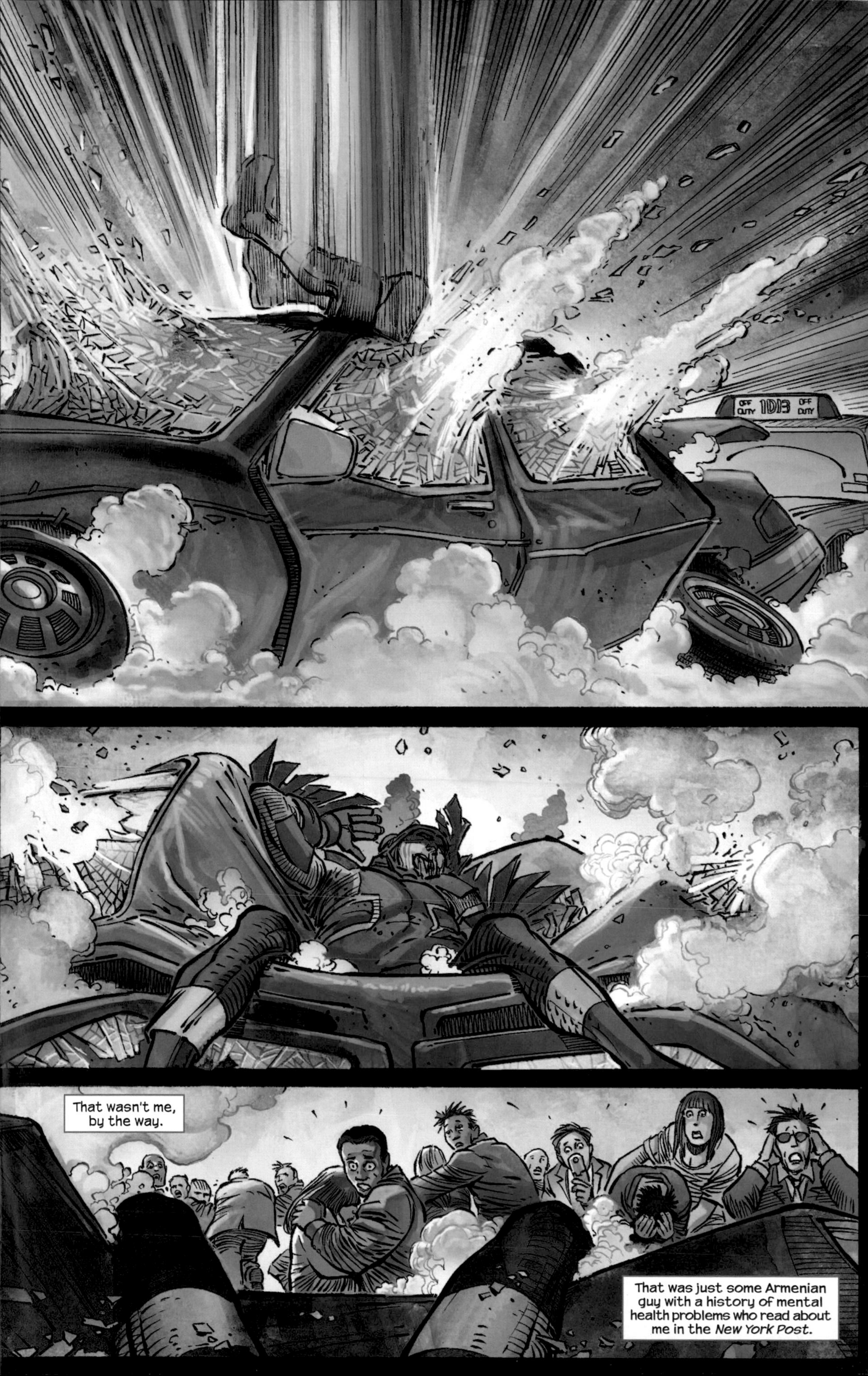
OFF DUTY 1D13 OFF DUTY
That wasn't me, by the way.
That was just some Armenian guy with a history of mental health problems who read about me in the *New York Post*.

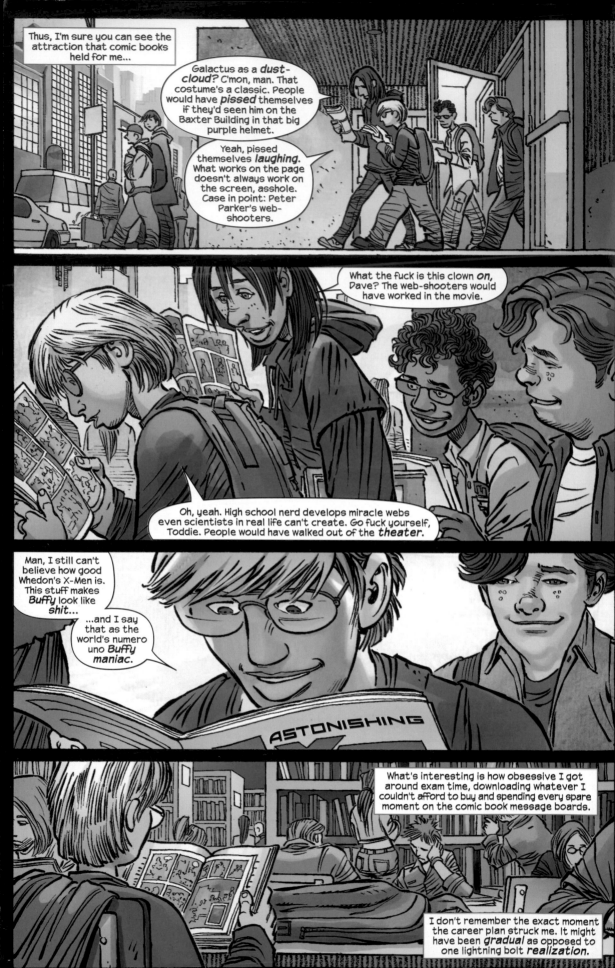

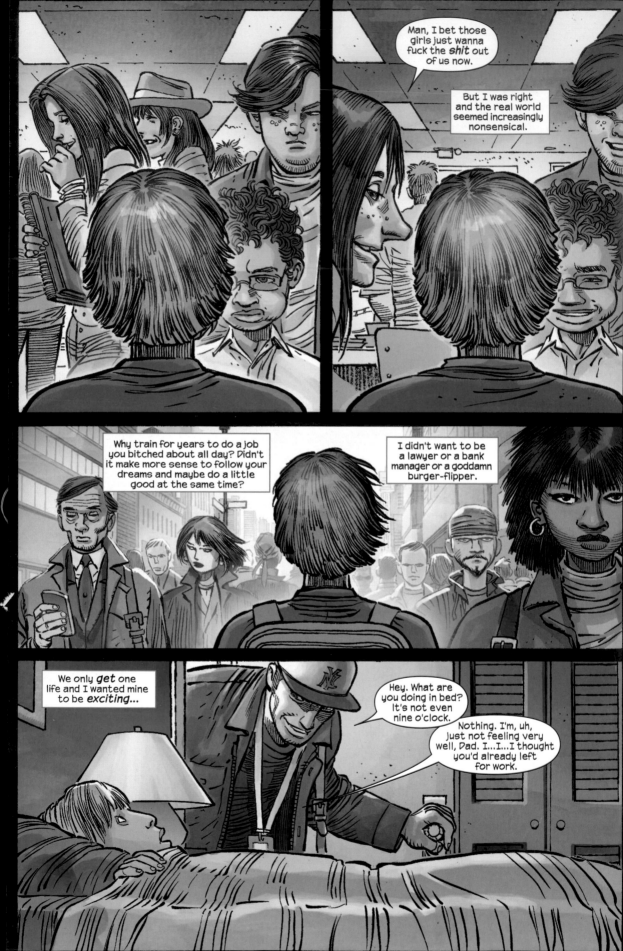

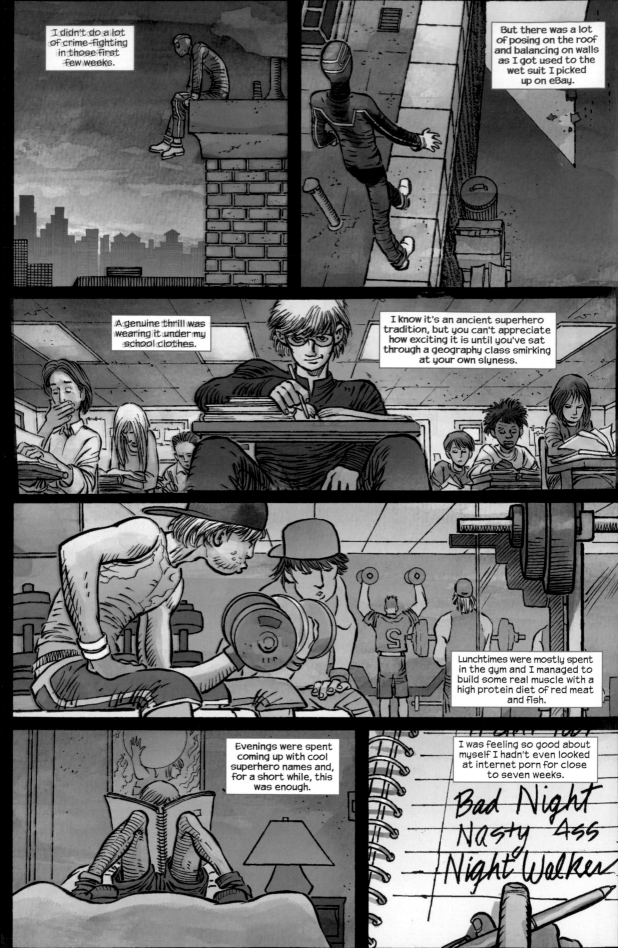

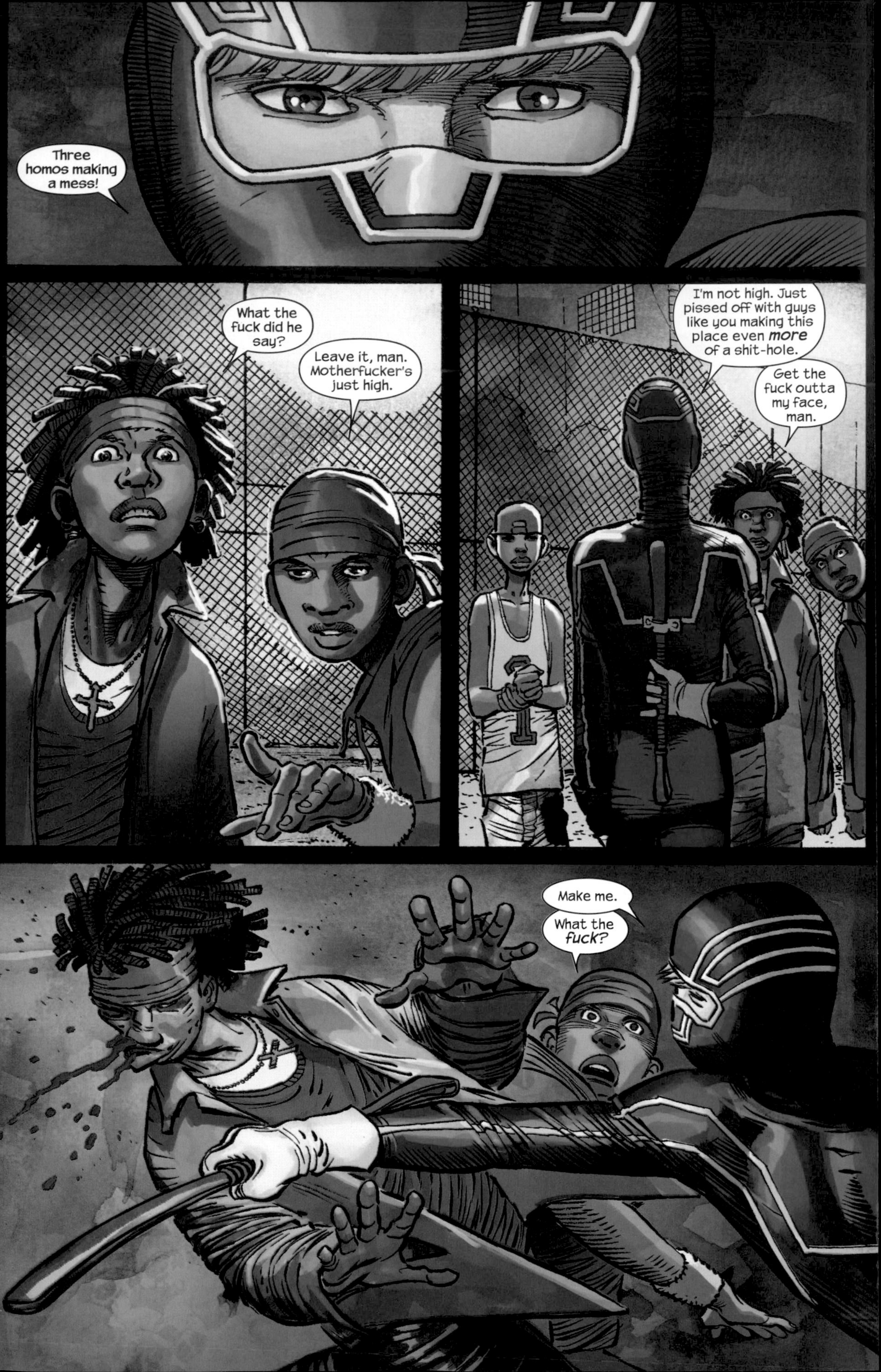

Three homos making a mess!
What the fuck did he say?
Leave it, man. Motherfucker's just high.
I'm not high. Just pissed off with guys like you making this place even *more* of a shit-hole.
Get the fuck outta my face, man.
Make me.
What the *fuck*?

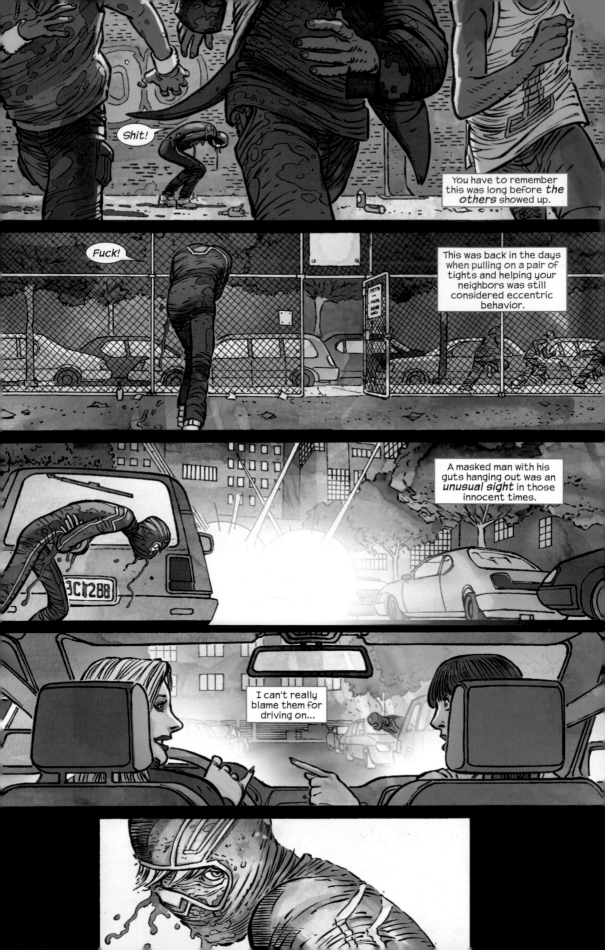

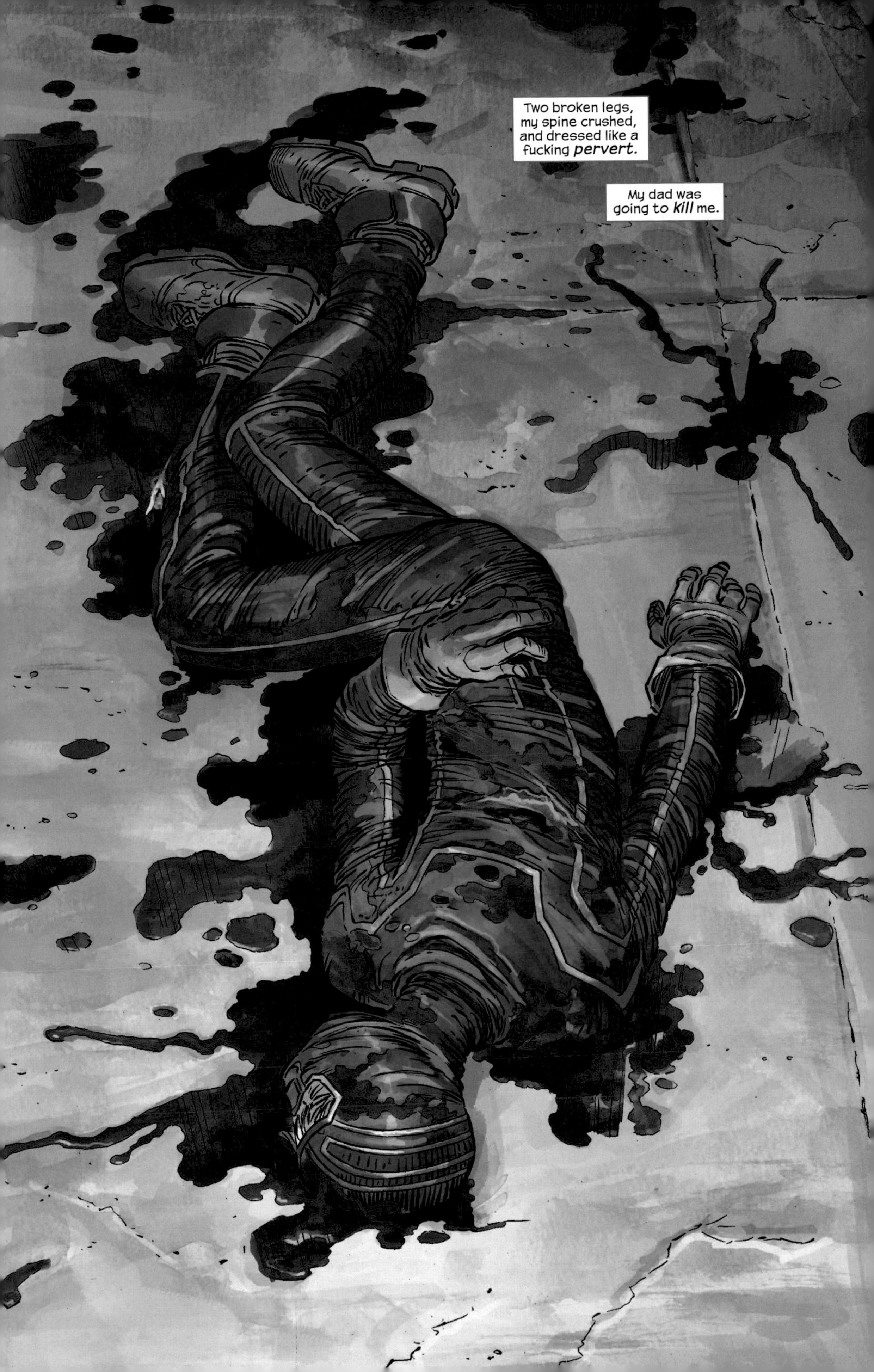
Two broken legs, my spine crushed, and dressed like a fucking *pervert*.
My dad was going to *kill* me.

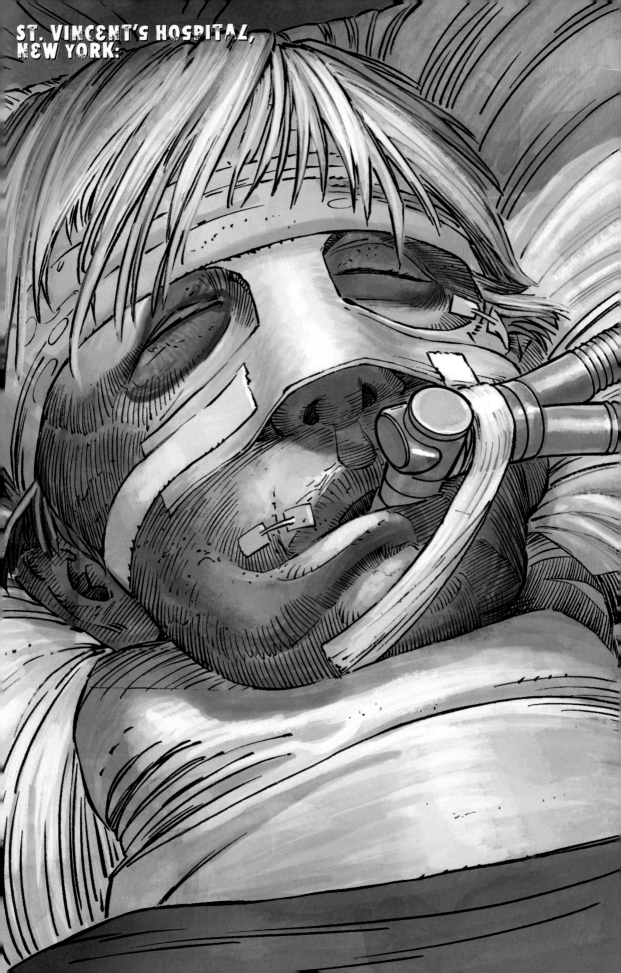

ST. VINCENT'S HOSPITAL,
NEW YORK:

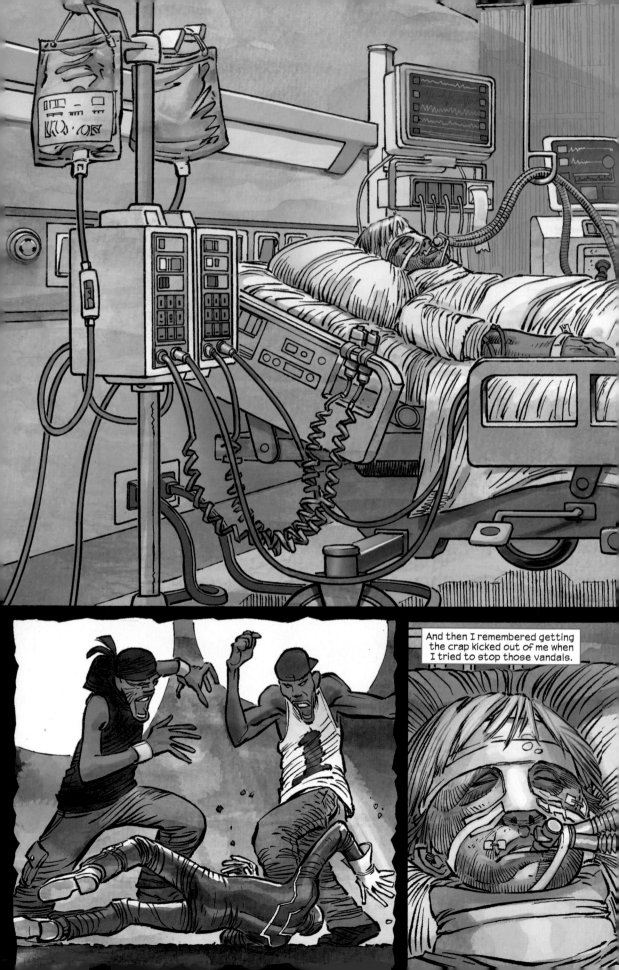

And then I remembered getting the crap kicked out of me when I tried to stop those vandals.

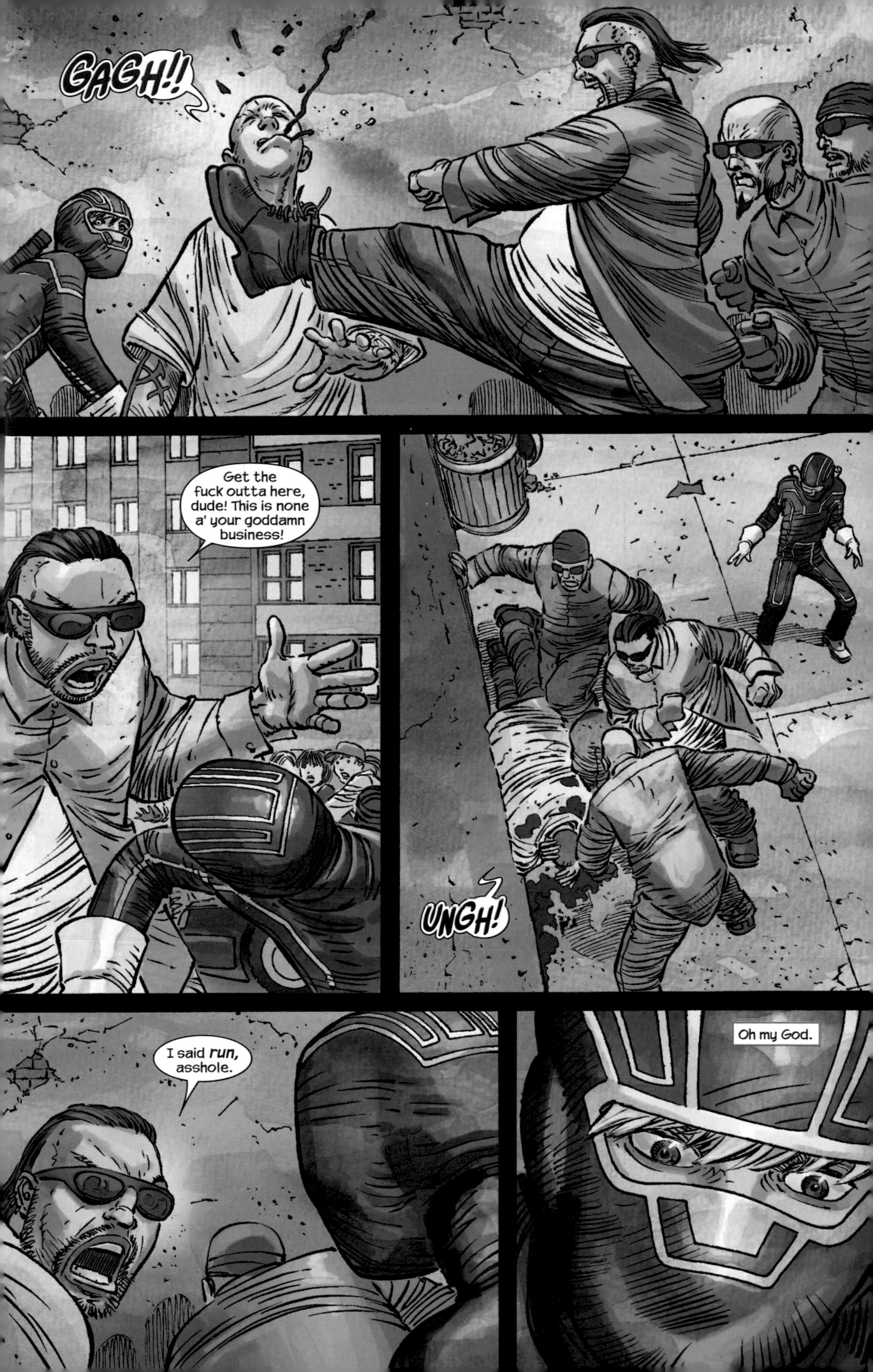
GAGH!!
Get the fuck outta here, dude! This is none a' your goddamn business!
UNGH!
I said *run,* asshole.
Oh my God.

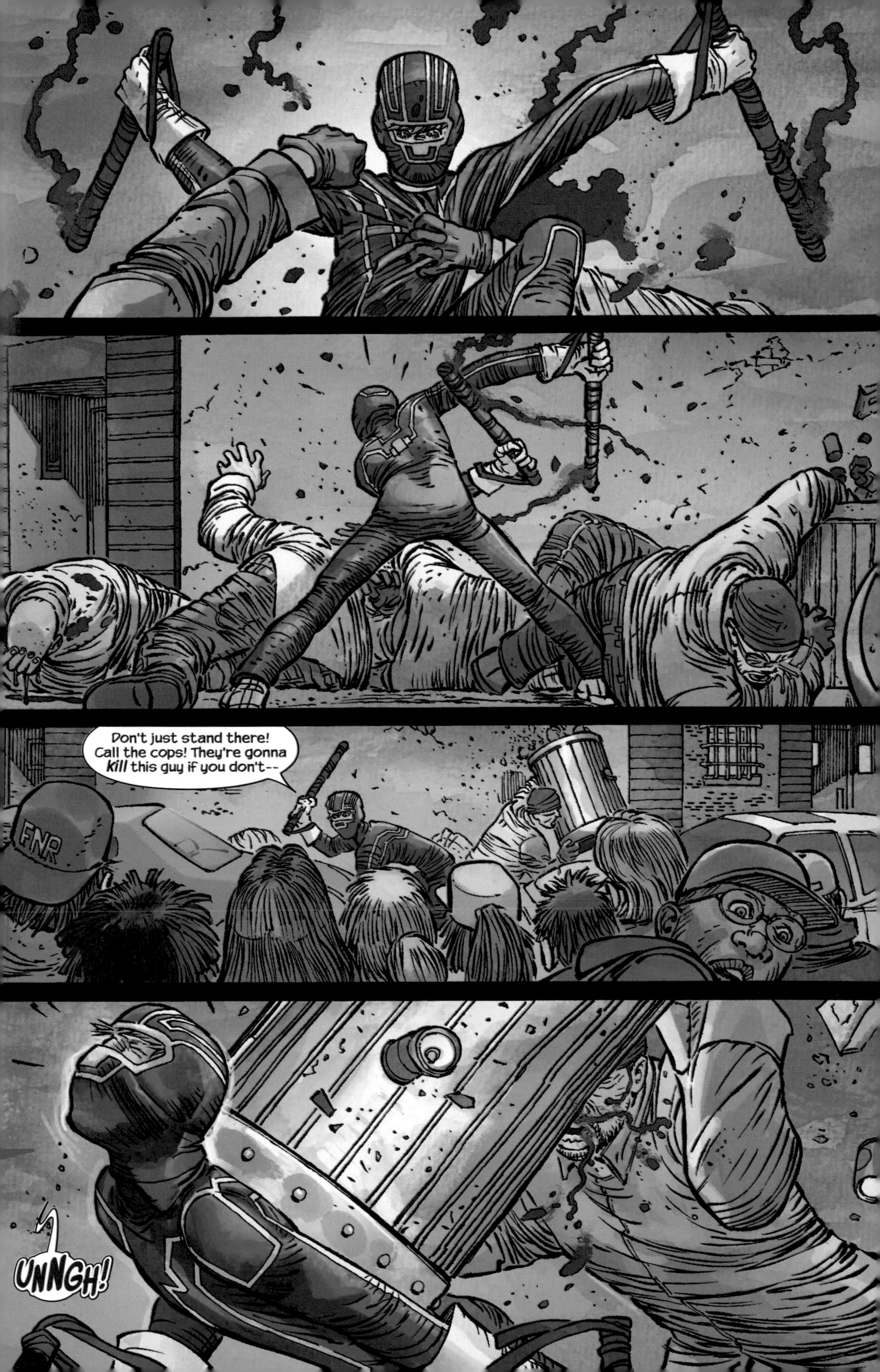
Don't just stand there! Call the cops! They're gonna *kill* this guy if you don't--
FNR
UNNGH!

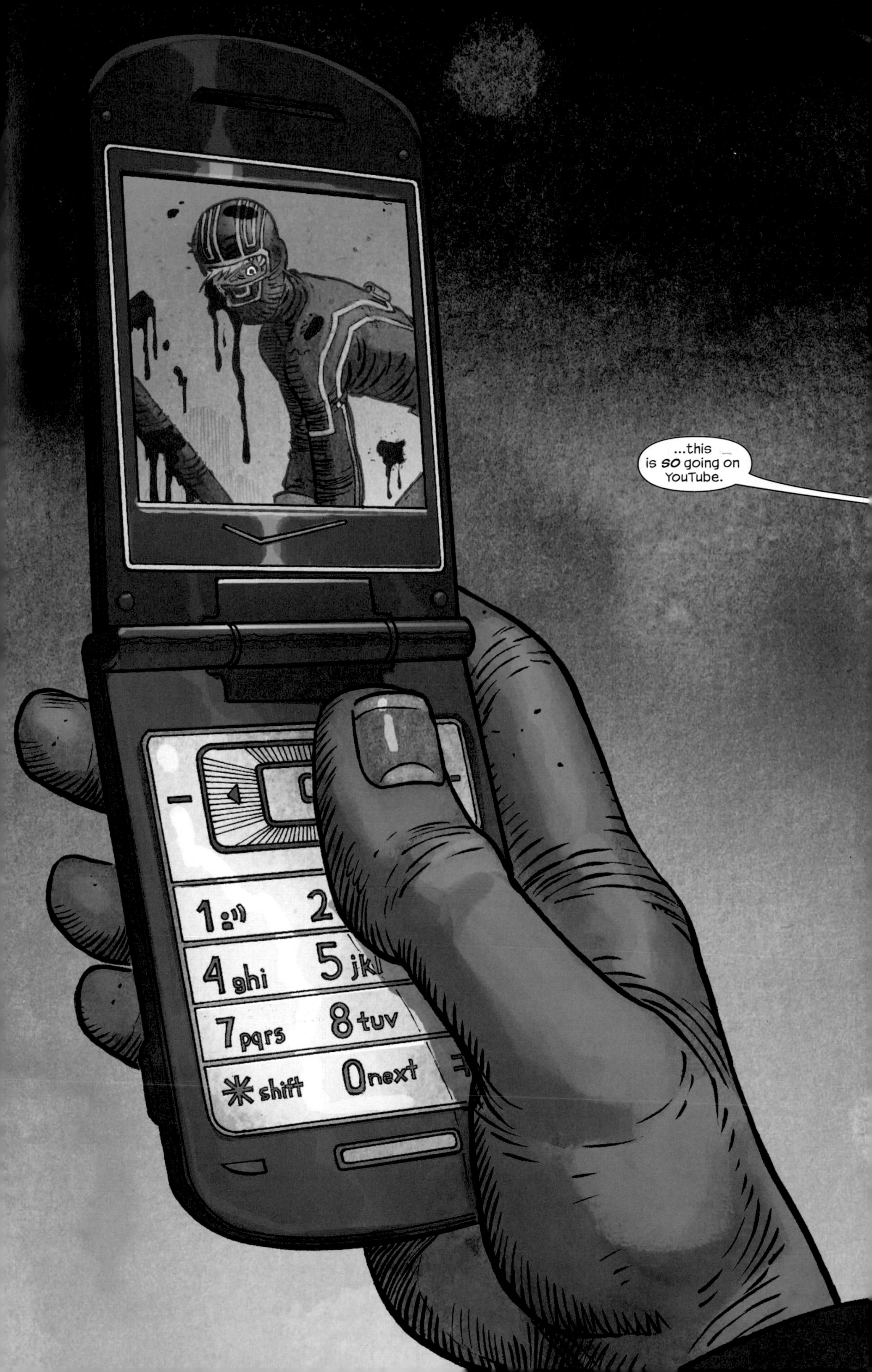
...this is *SO* going on YouTube.
1 2
4 ghi 5 jkl
7 pqrs 8 tuv
* shift 0 next

Kick-Ass

Oh, man. This is that video on the news last night. The guy who saved that kid from those *muggers?*

I'm not leaving him! You hear me?

I'm not **leaving** him...

This is fucking great. Is he really wearing a superhero costume?

You wouldn't believe how fast the celebrity thing happened.

All it took was my fight with those Puerto Ricans to get online and suddenly I was everywhere.

I was the little guy who refused to give up. The world's first real-life superhero.

Jay Leno said I was an *inspiration*. David Letterman gave me a *salute* at the end of his show.

I was a global sensation inside twenty-four hours. A bad-ass version of the Star Wars Kid. It was the greatest moment of my entire life...

KICK-ASS!

...and I finally had a name.

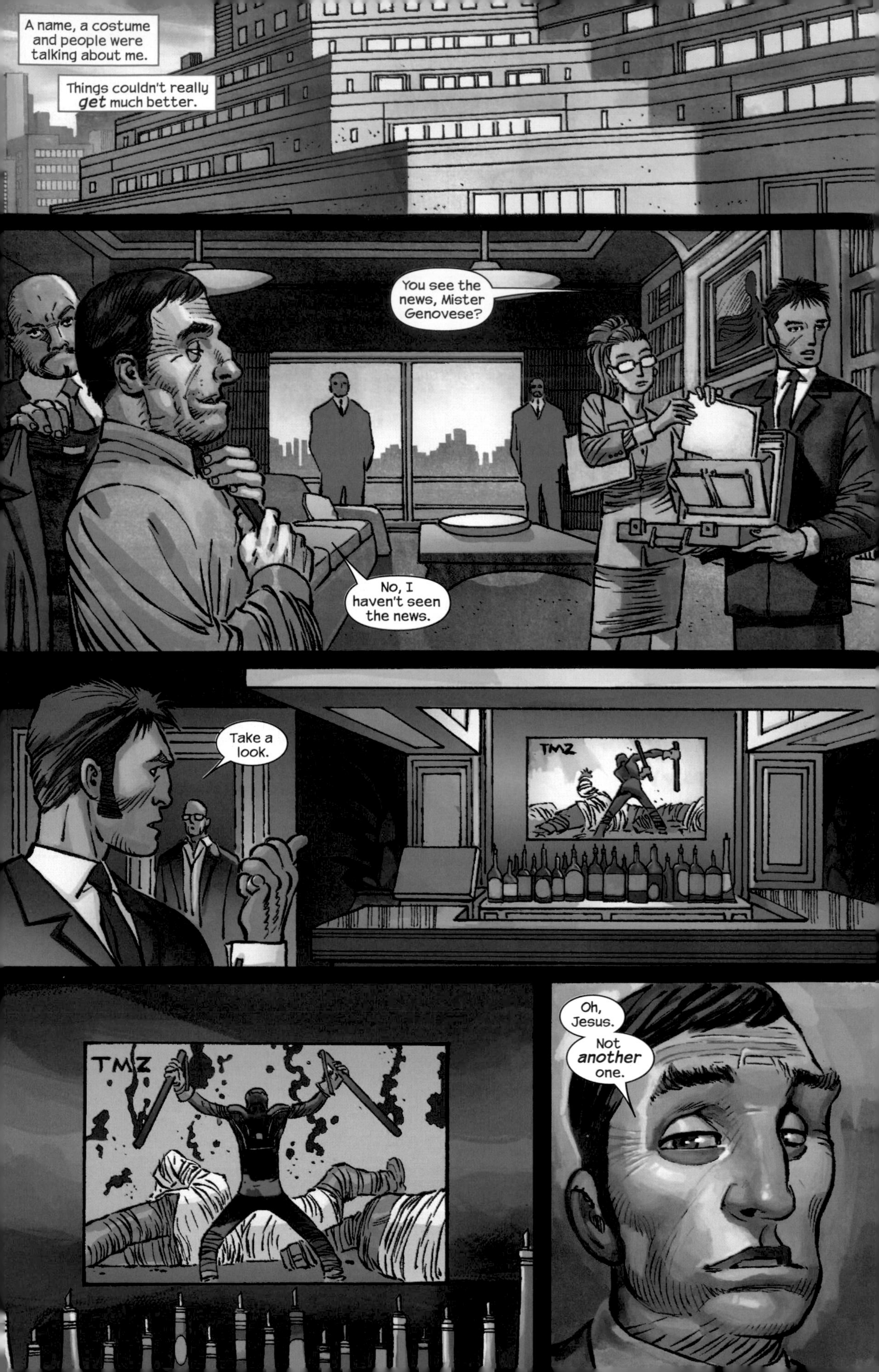
A name, a costume and people were talking about me.
Things couldn't really *get* much better.
You see the news, Mister Genovese?
No, I haven't seen the news.
Take a look.
TMZ
TMZ
Oh, Jesus.
Not *another* one.

I figured that was the difference between comic books and real life. Real superheroes were down where the *action* was...

Kick-Ass!

Hey, dude!

WE LOVE YOU, YOU CRAZY MOTHER-FUCKER!

Cool!

I'd started a MySpace page so people with problems could get in touch and I could maybe help them out a little.

It seemed a more effective way of doing the job than just wandering around on patrol every night.

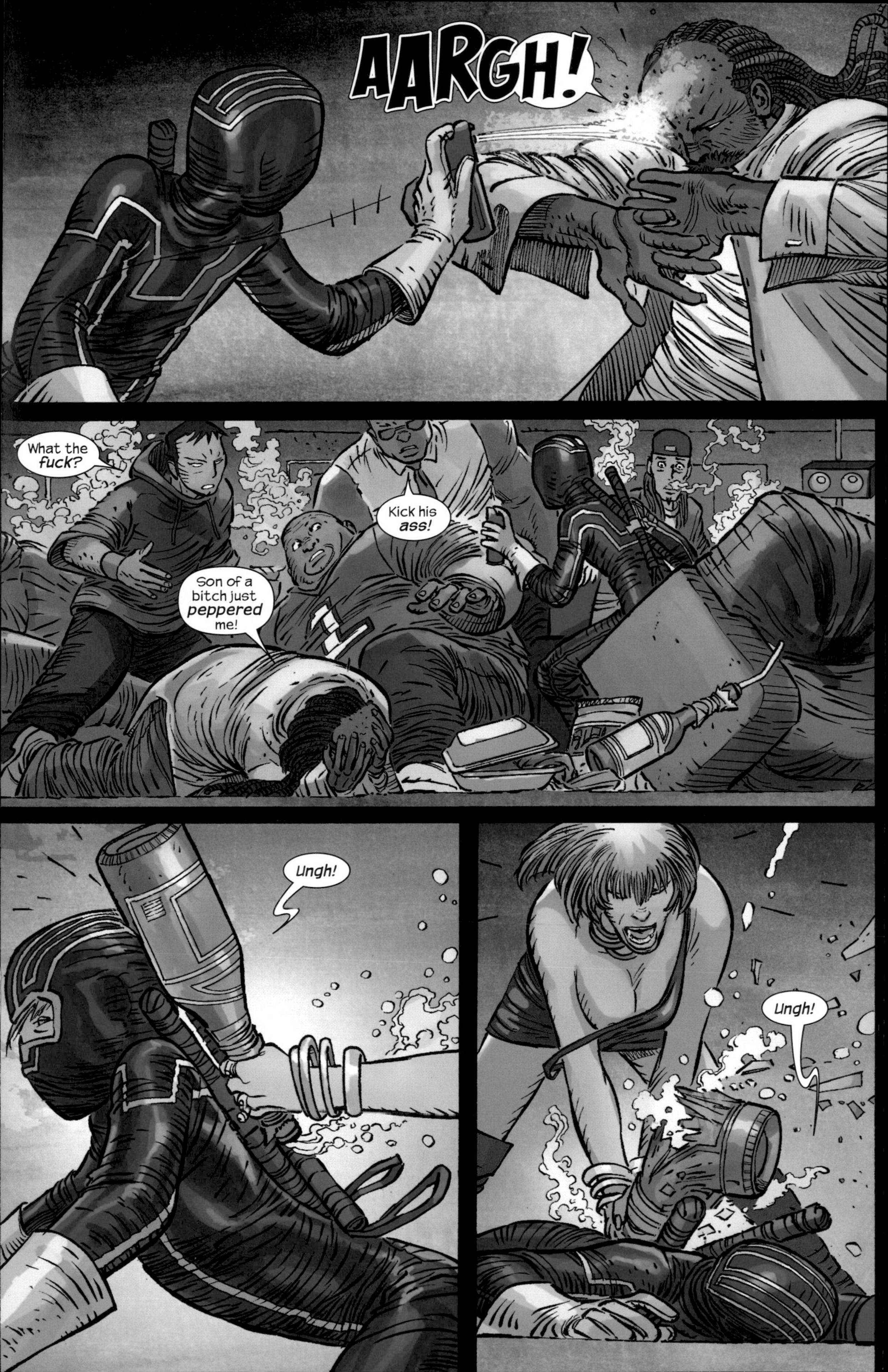
AARGH!
What the fuck?
Kick his ass!
Son of a bitch just peppered me!
Ungh!
Ungh!

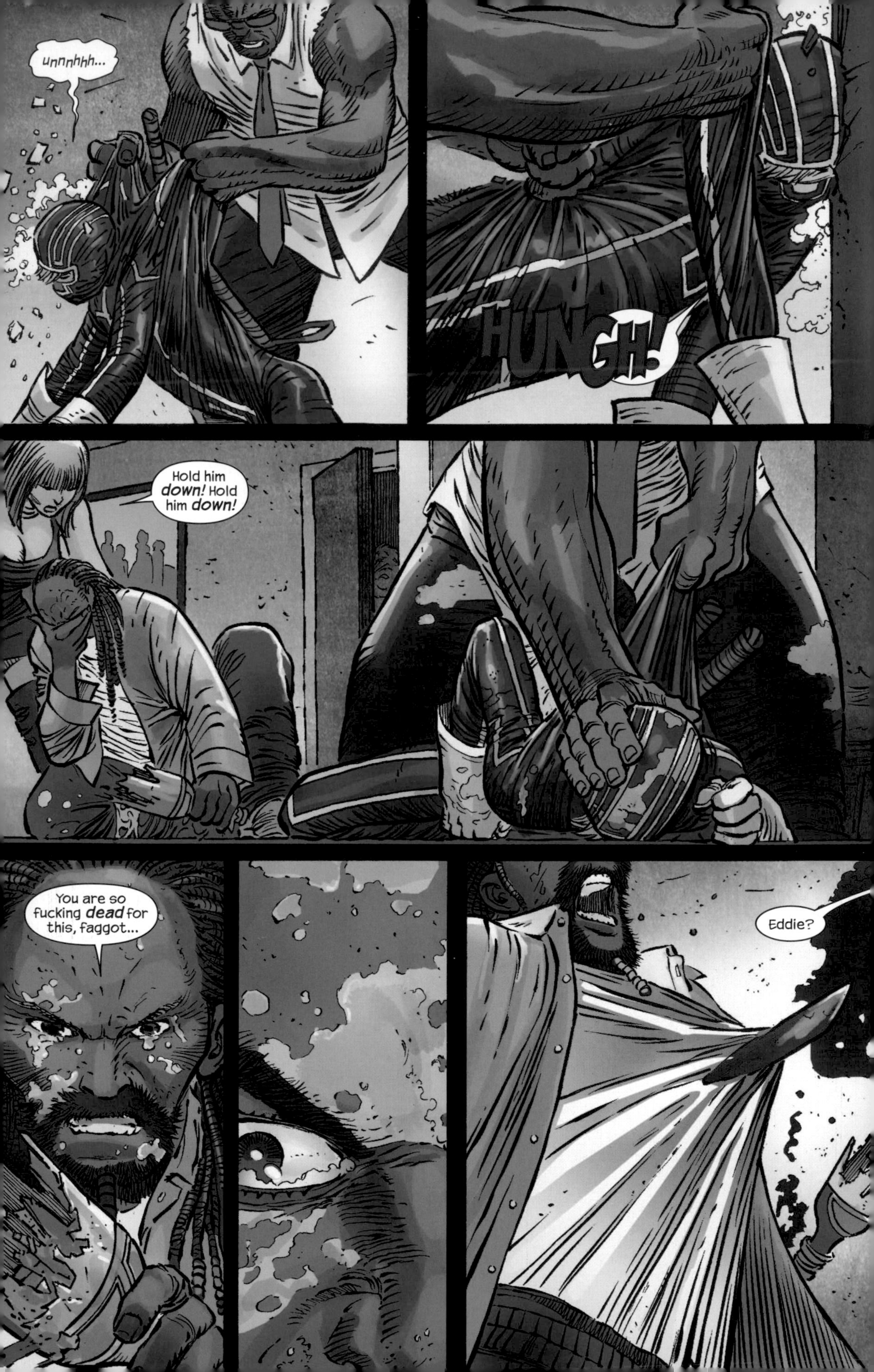
unnnhhh...
HUNGH!
Hold him *down!* Hold him *down!*
You are so fucking ***dead*** for this, faggot...
Eddie?

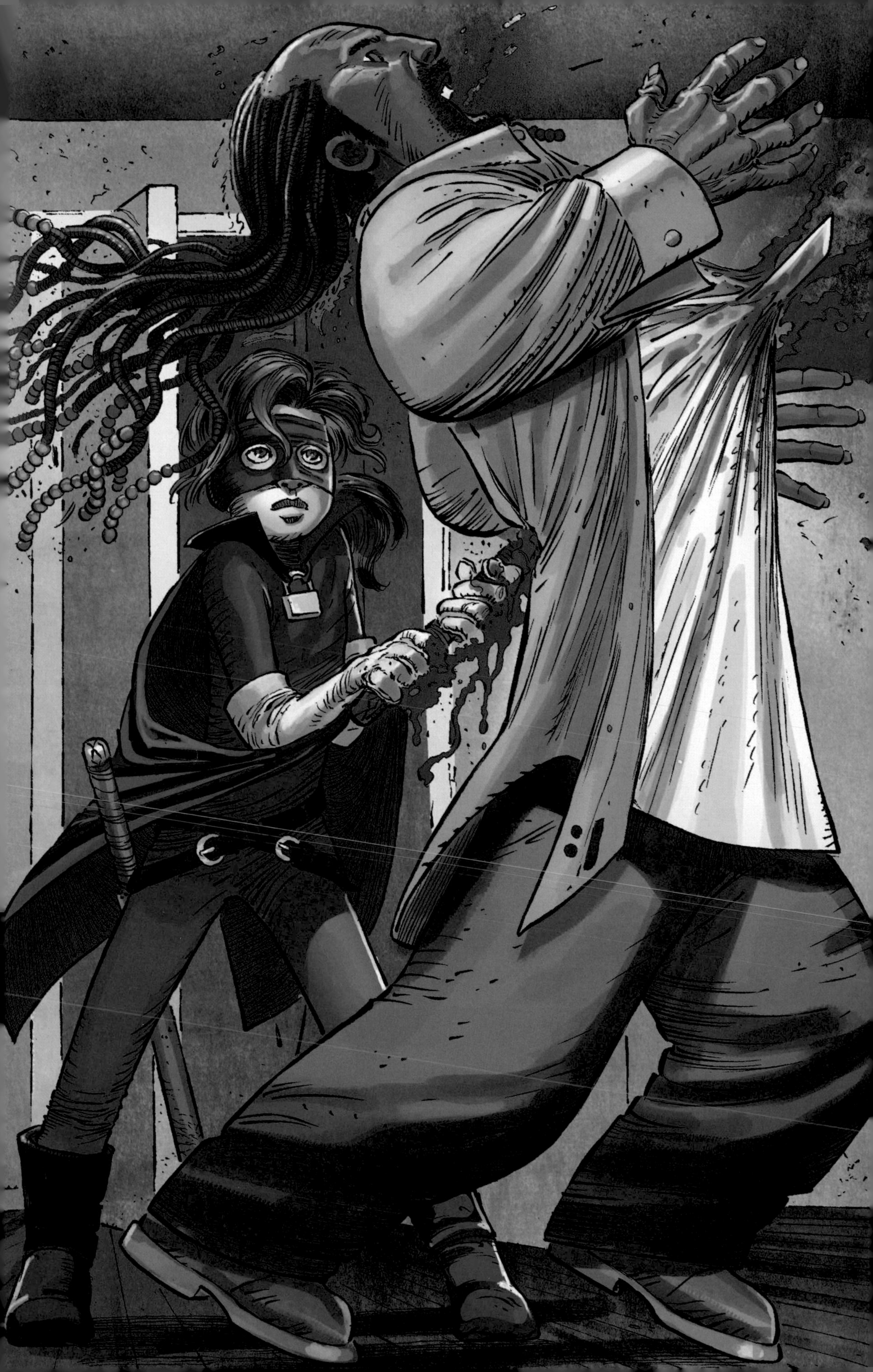

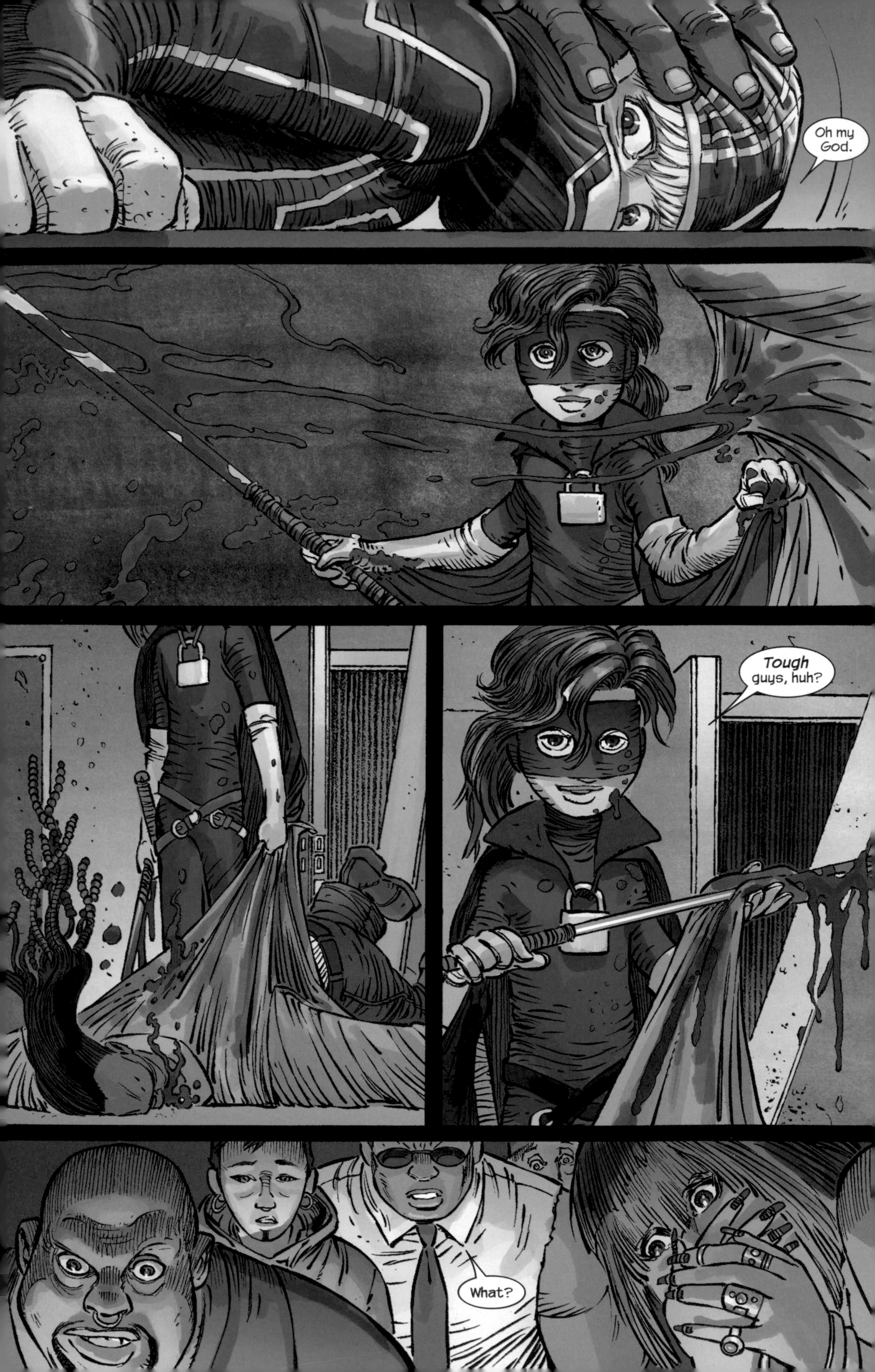
Oh my God.
Tough guys, huh?
What?

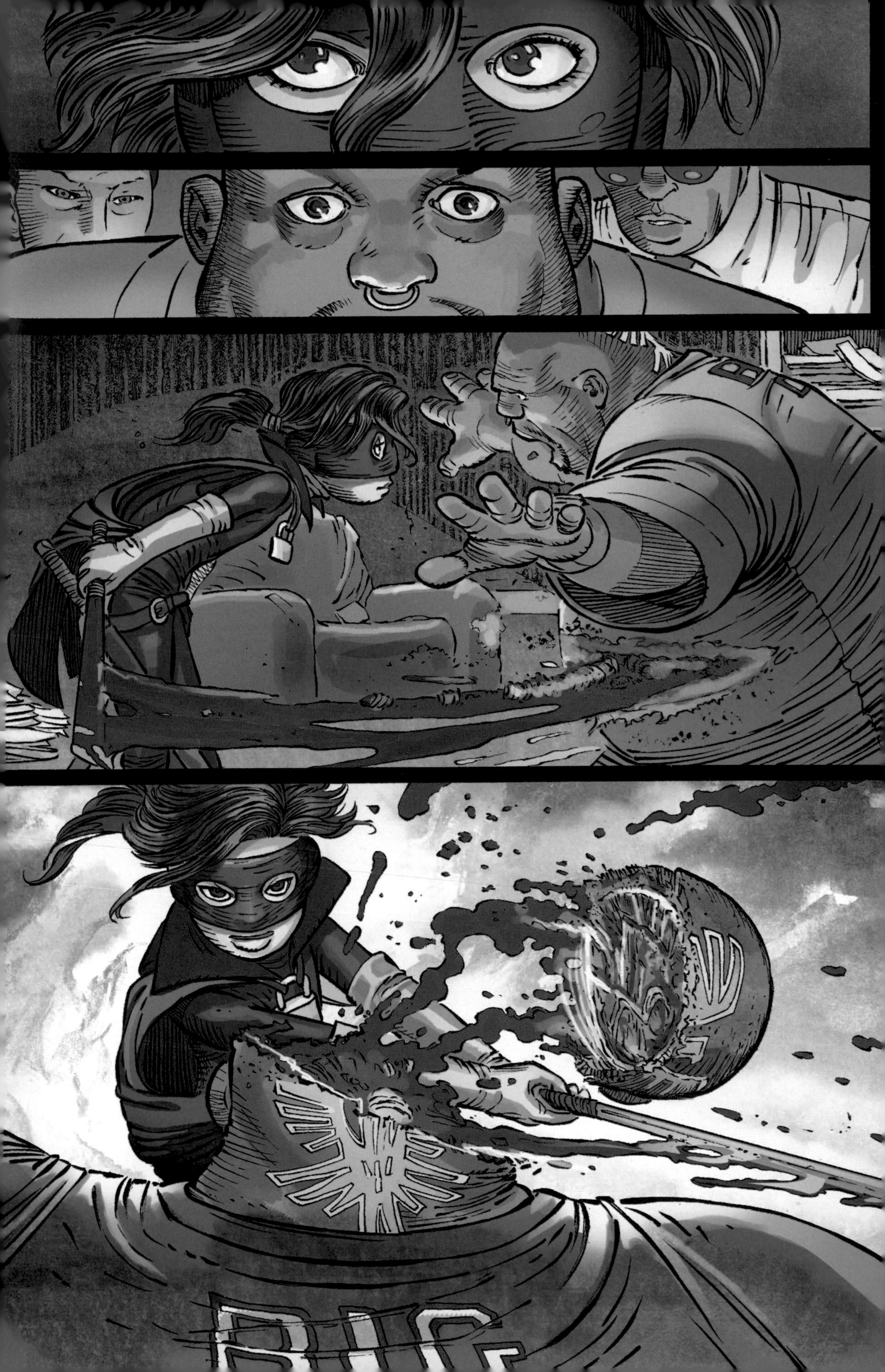

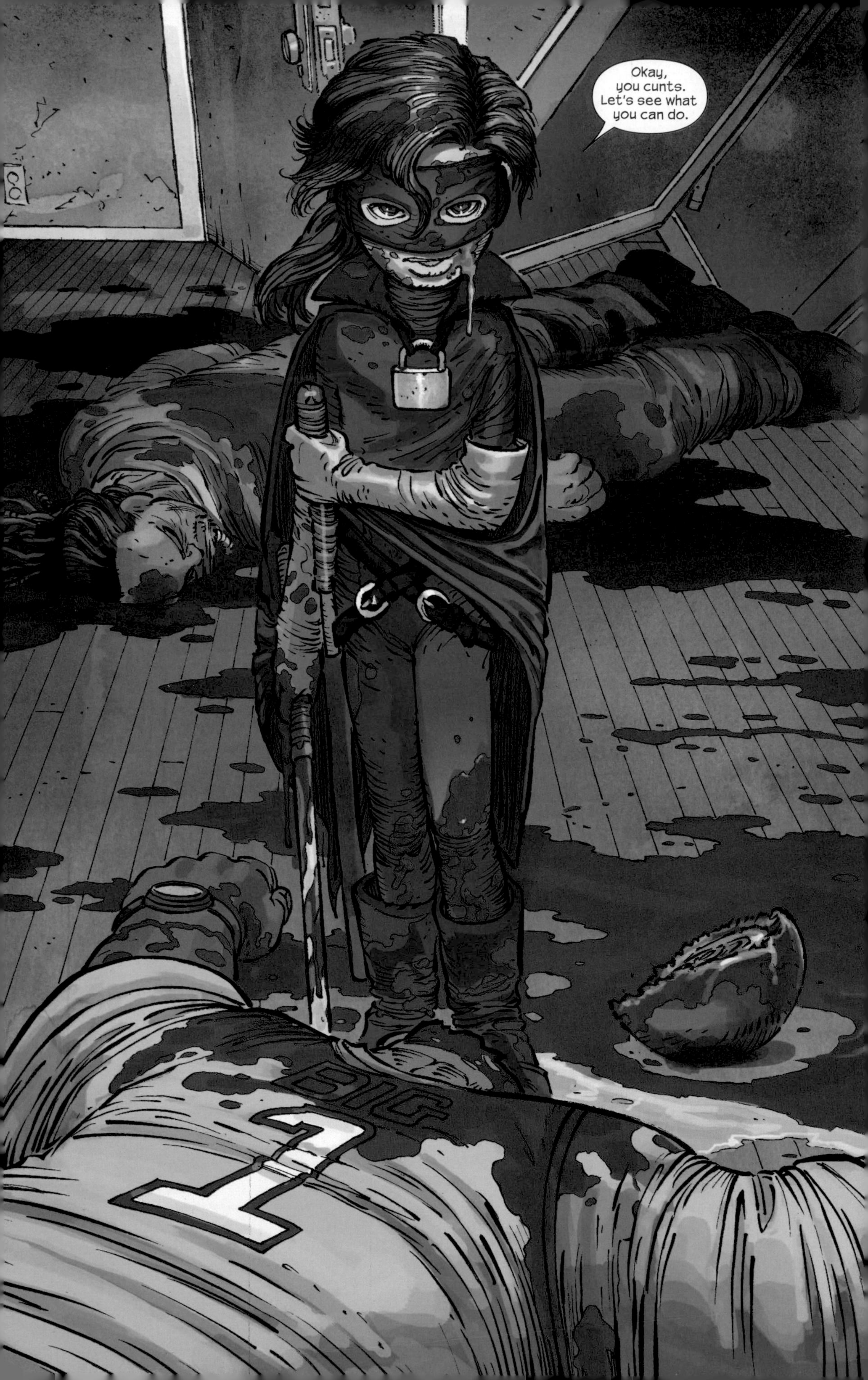
Okay, you cunts. Let's see what you can do.
BIG

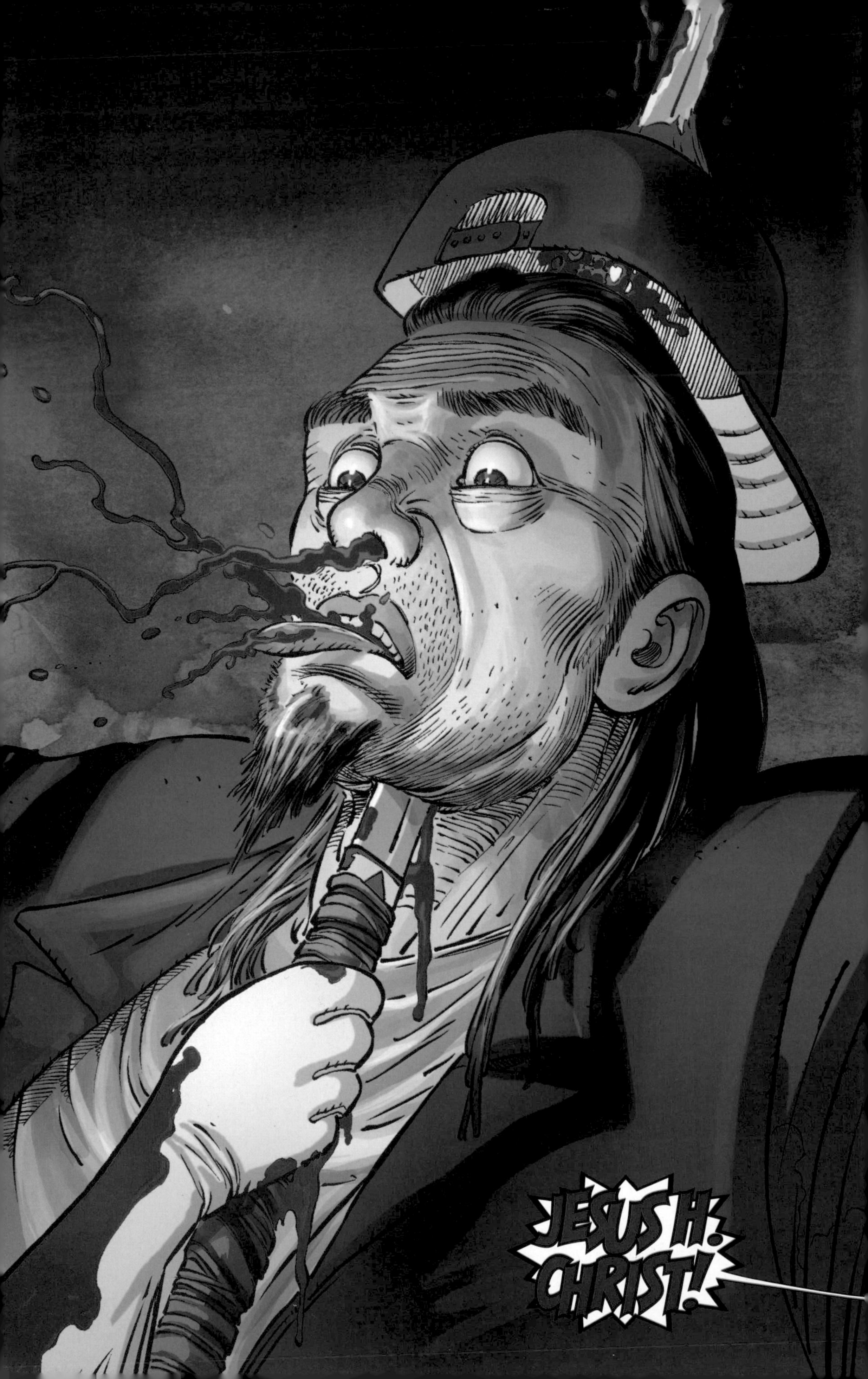
JESUS H. CHRIST!

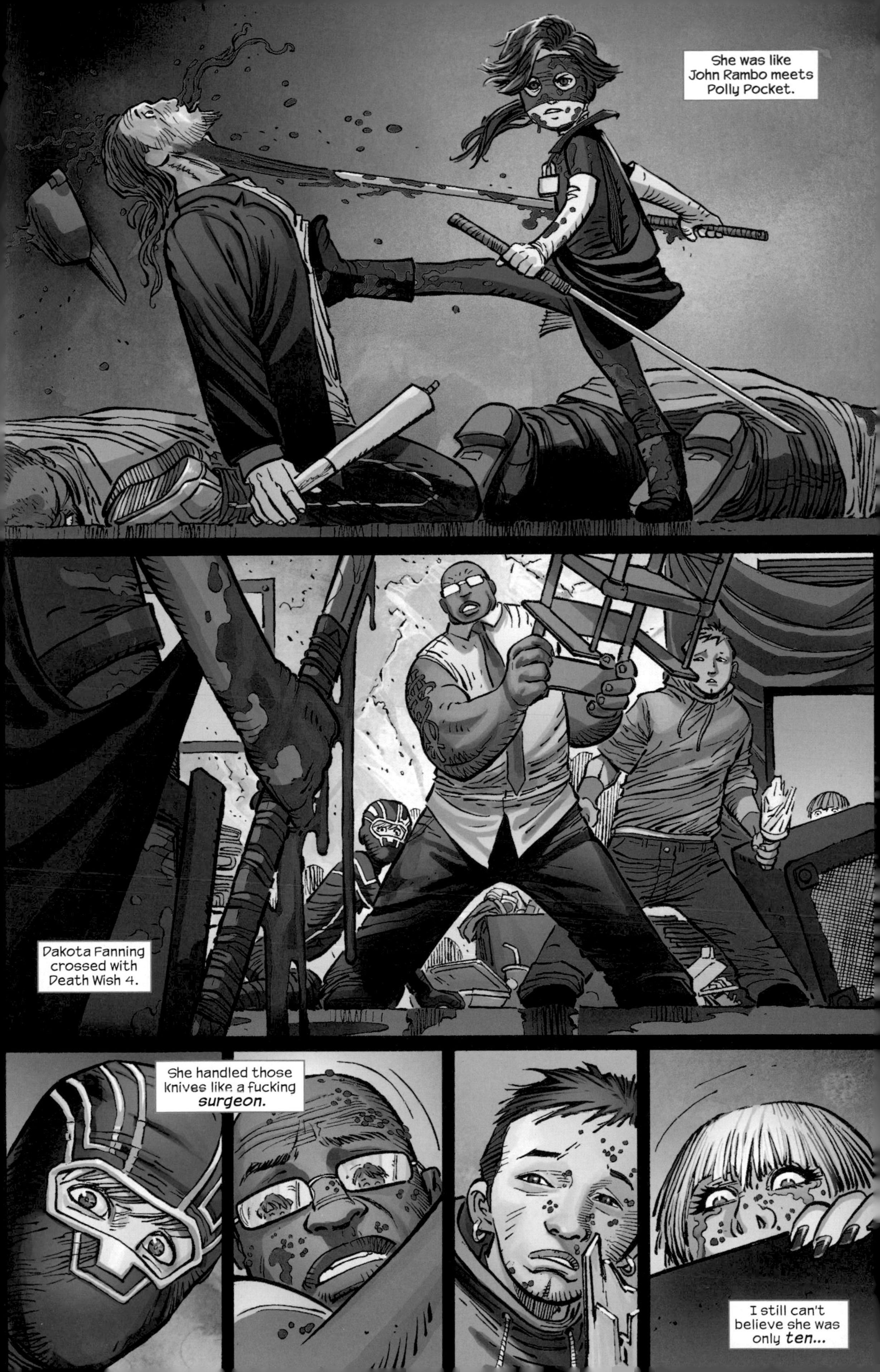
She was like John Rambo meets Polly Pocket.
Dakota Fanning crossed with Death Wish 4.
She handled those knives like a fucking *surgeon.*
I still can't believe she was only *ten...*

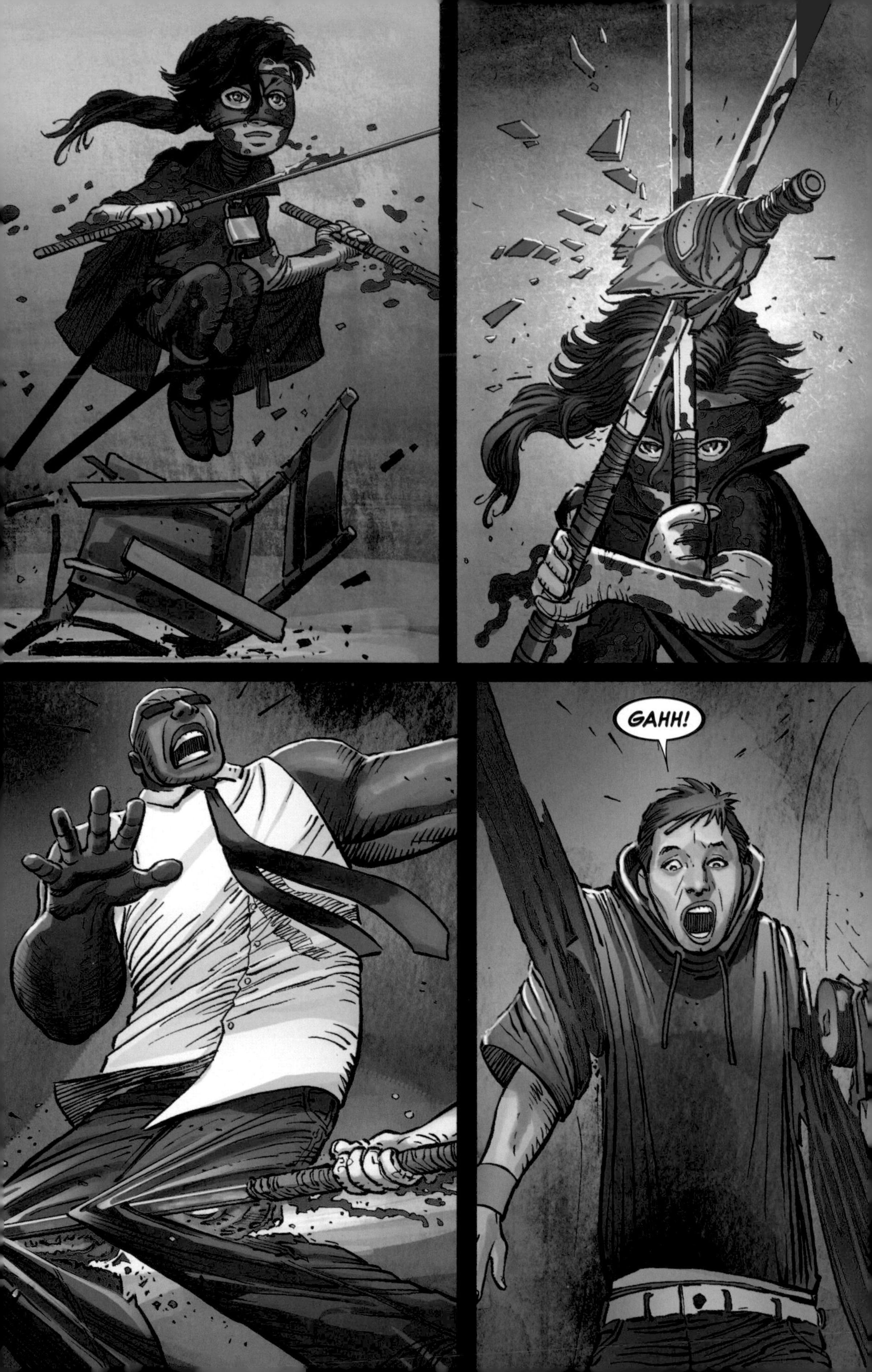
GAHH!

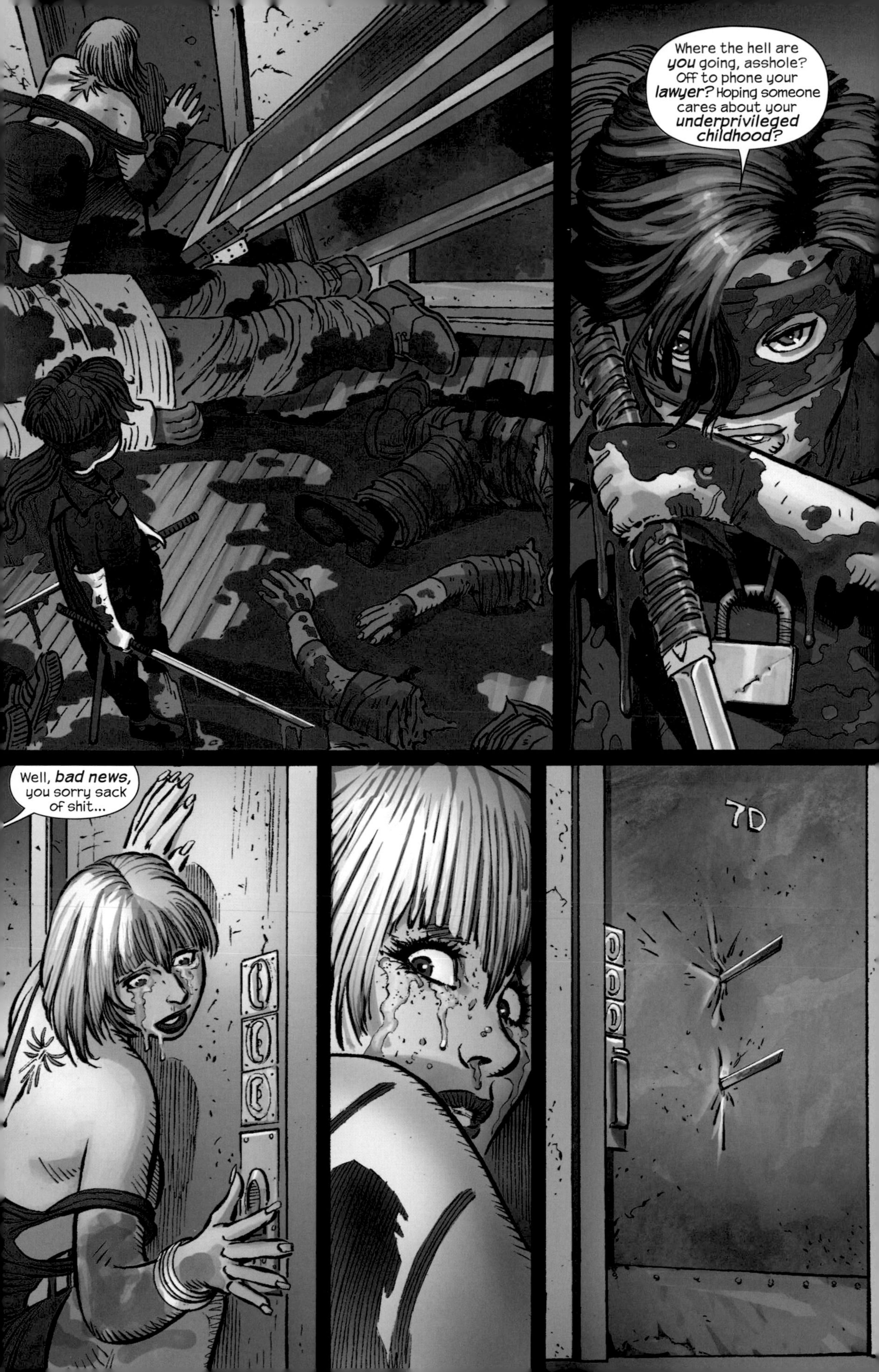
Where the hell are you going, asshole? Off to phone your lawyer? Hoping someone cares about your underprivileged childhood?
Well, bad news, you sorry sack of shit...
7D

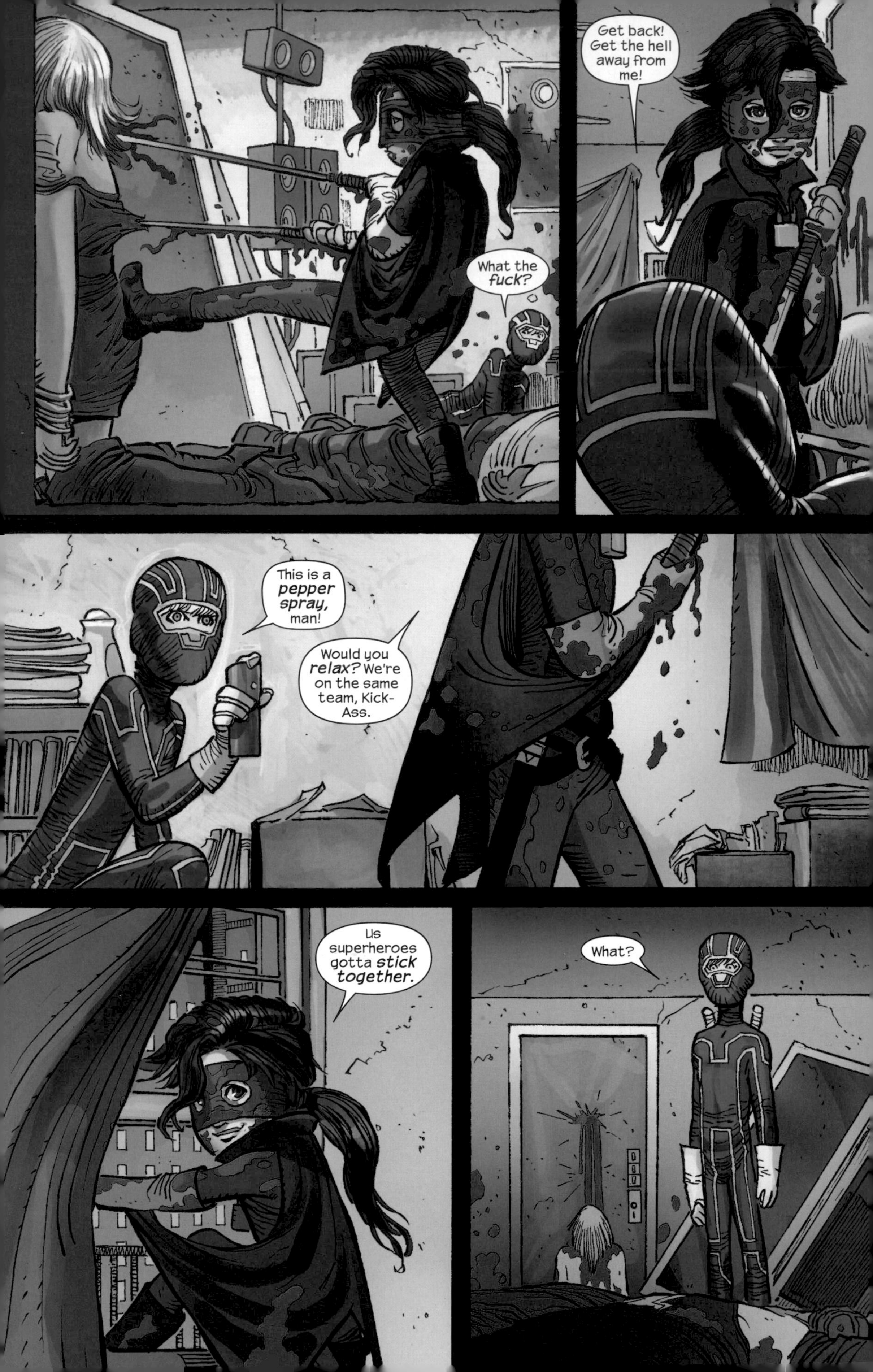
What the *fuck?*
Get back! Get the hell away from me!
This is a **pepper spray,** man!
Would you **relax?** We're on the same team, Kick-Ass.
Us superheroes gotta **stick together.**
What?

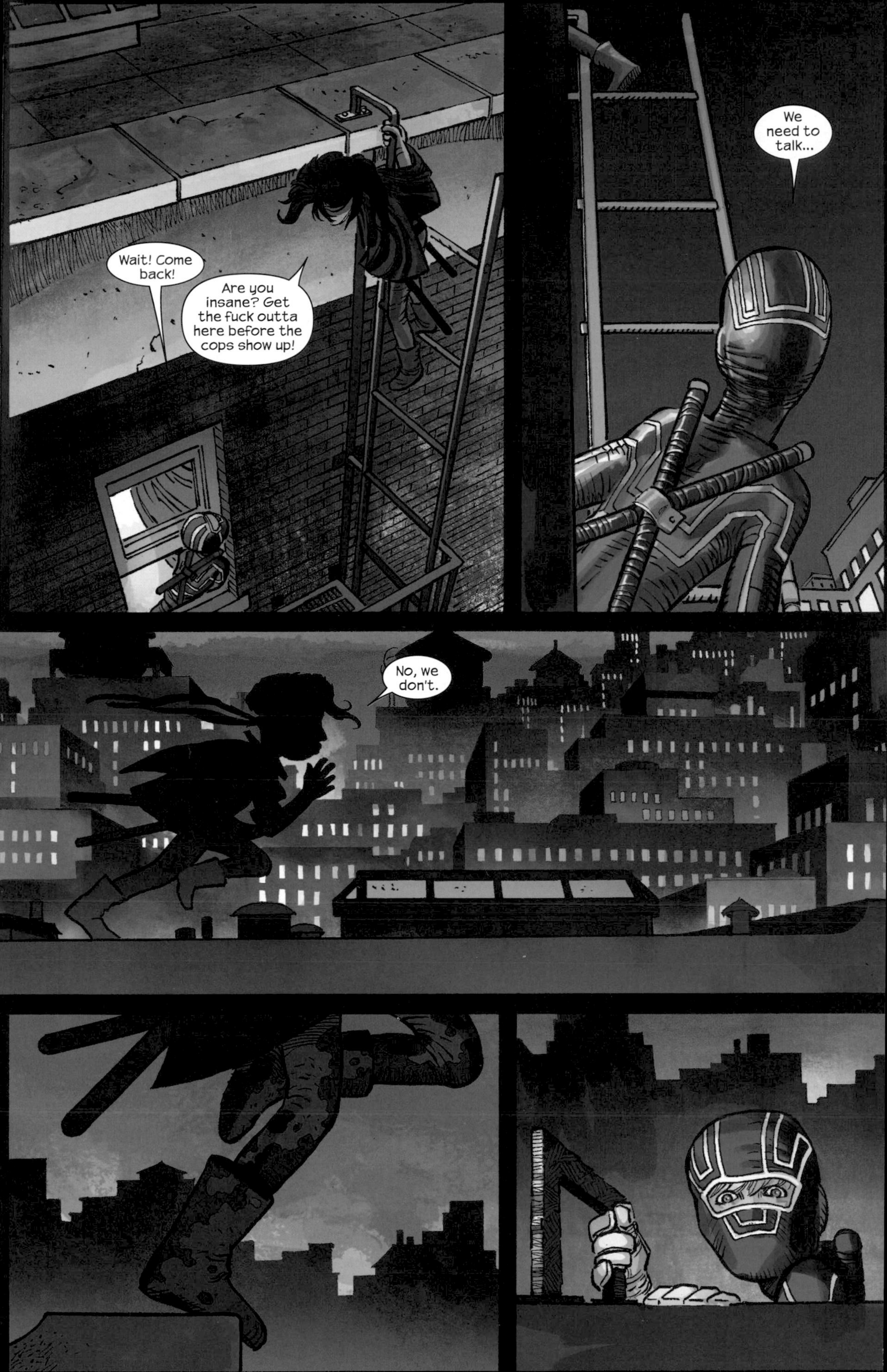
Wait! Come back!
Are you insane? Get the fuck outta here before the cops show up!
We need to talk...
No, we don't.

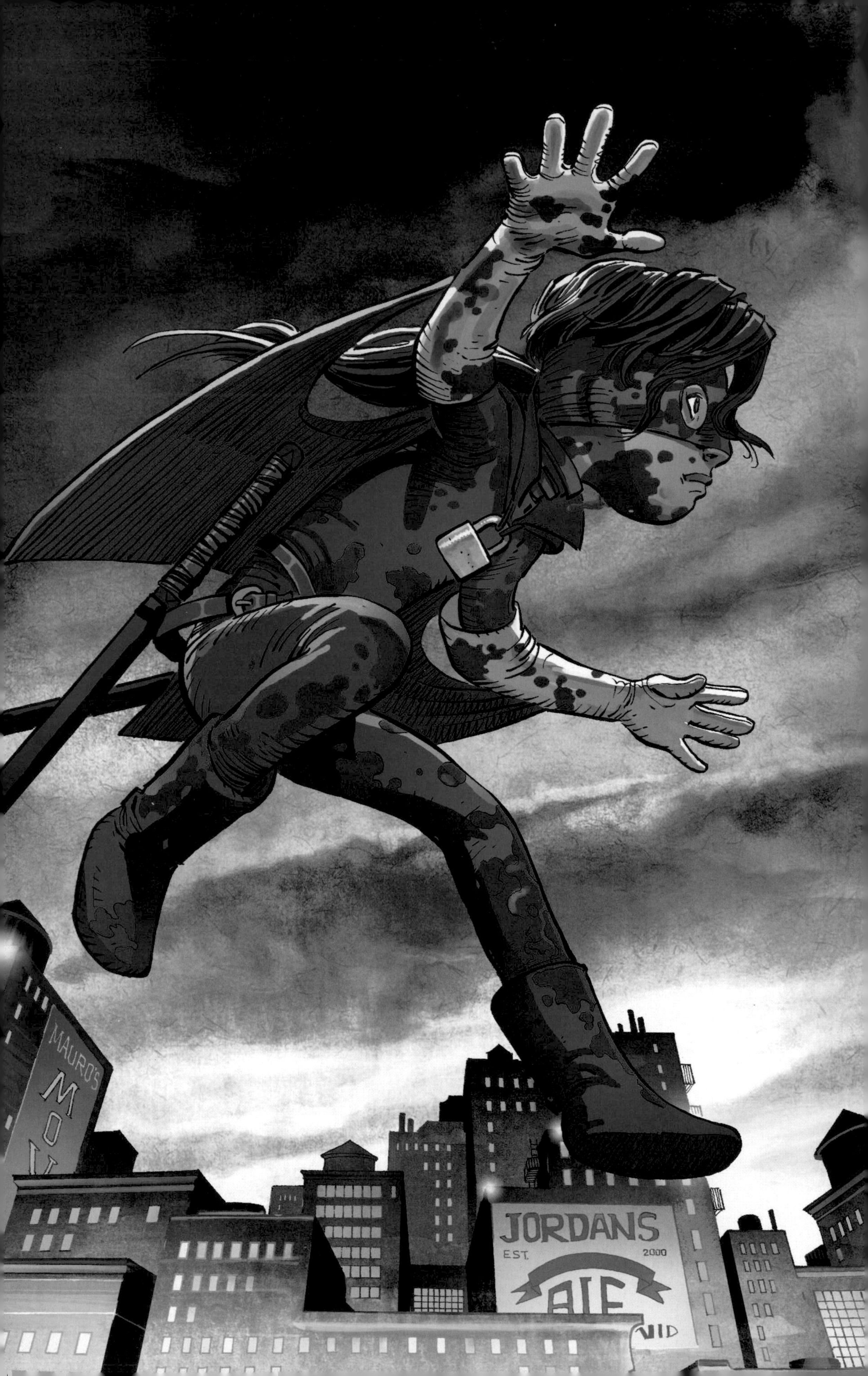
MAURO'S
MOV
JORDANS
EST.
2000
ALE
VID

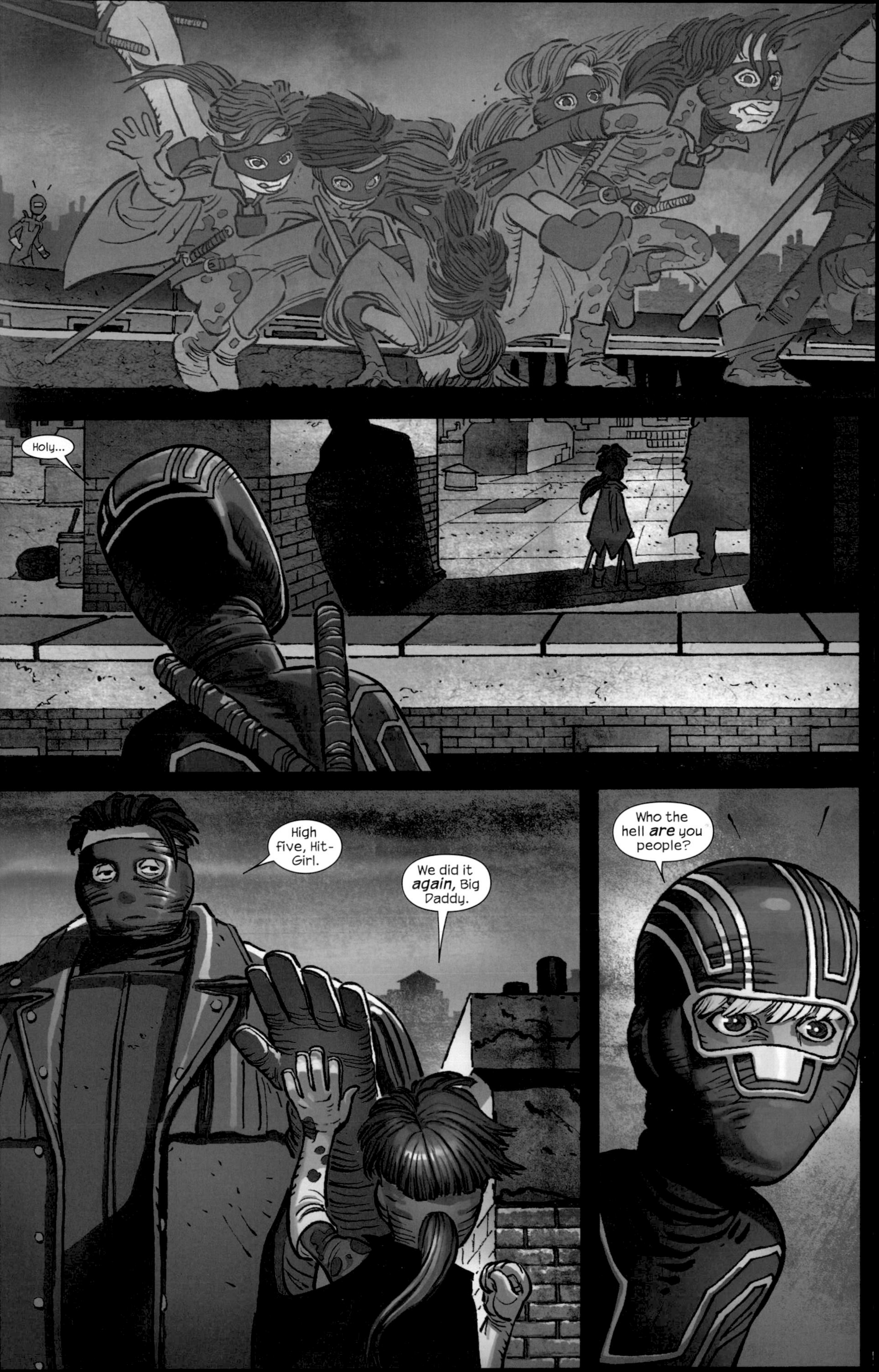

Holy...
High five, Hit-Girl.
We did it again, Big Daddy.
Who the hell are you people?

Sure, Dad. No problem.

...but as luck would have it I wasn't even *mentioned.*

Turns out Eddie Lomas was a well-known dealer and the cops said their deaths were the latest in a *turf war.*

I wouldn't say I was *happy...delirious* is more accurate...but I had to let his ex know what really went down.

It was twenty-four hours before the killings went public. Twenty-four *very long* fucking hours...

Just so she knew I had nothing to do with it...

Studio 347 HAIR SALON

347

Hell, no need to lie to *me,* Kick-Ass. World's a better place without *that* asshole.

347

No, you don't understand. It was these *other* superheroes. Some *big guy* and a crazy *little girl.*

Relax, honey. I gotcha. The cops don't need to know our *little secret.*

You and I never even had this conversation, right?

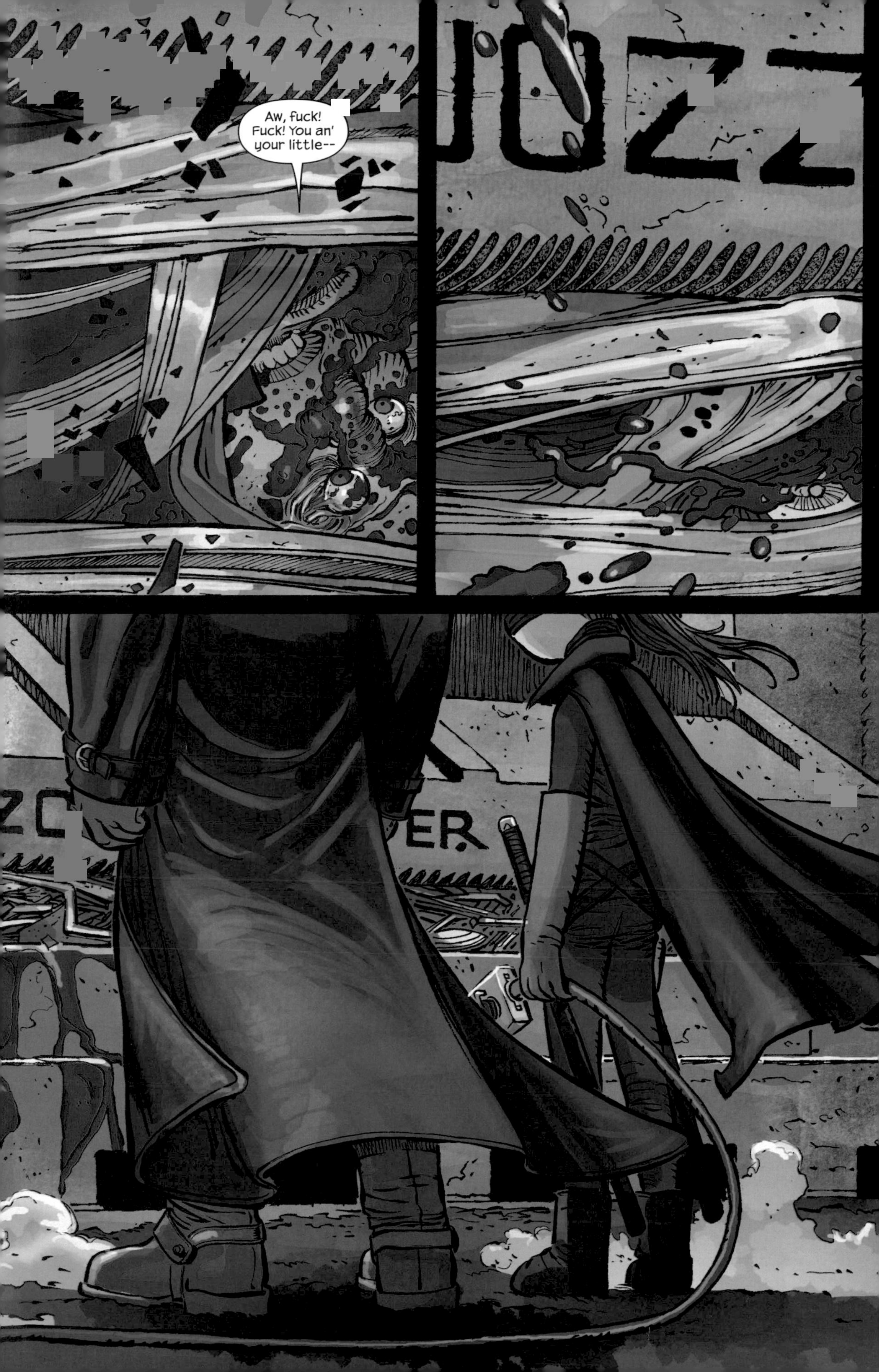
Aw, fuck! Fuck! You an' your little--

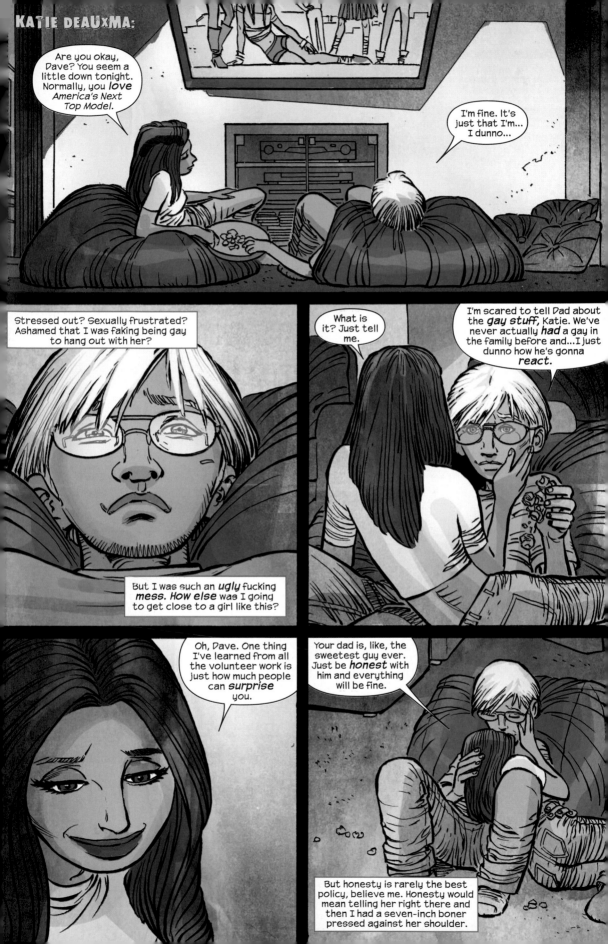

Where the hell do you get off saying you made up that *web-page* shit?

Oh, Jesus. Listen, you would not believe how much they *misquoted* me, man. I actually name-checked the hell out of you to those reporters.

What?

Seriously. This whole superhero thing's been bubbling away for years, but you were the first to get out there and have the balls to *do* it, man.

I'm your biggest fan. This is like meeting *Elvis* or something.

Uh, right. Well, it's nice to meet you too. *Cool outfit*, by the way.

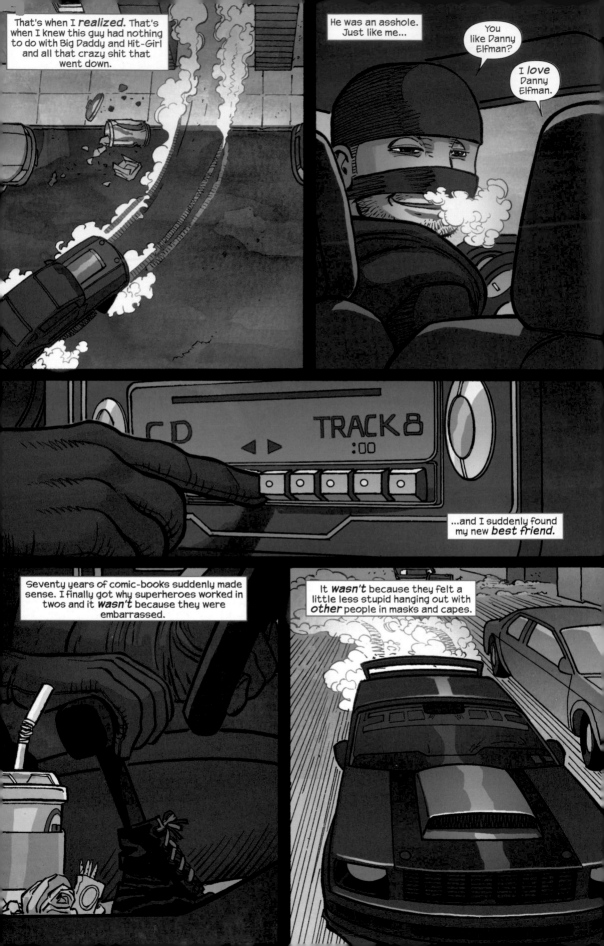

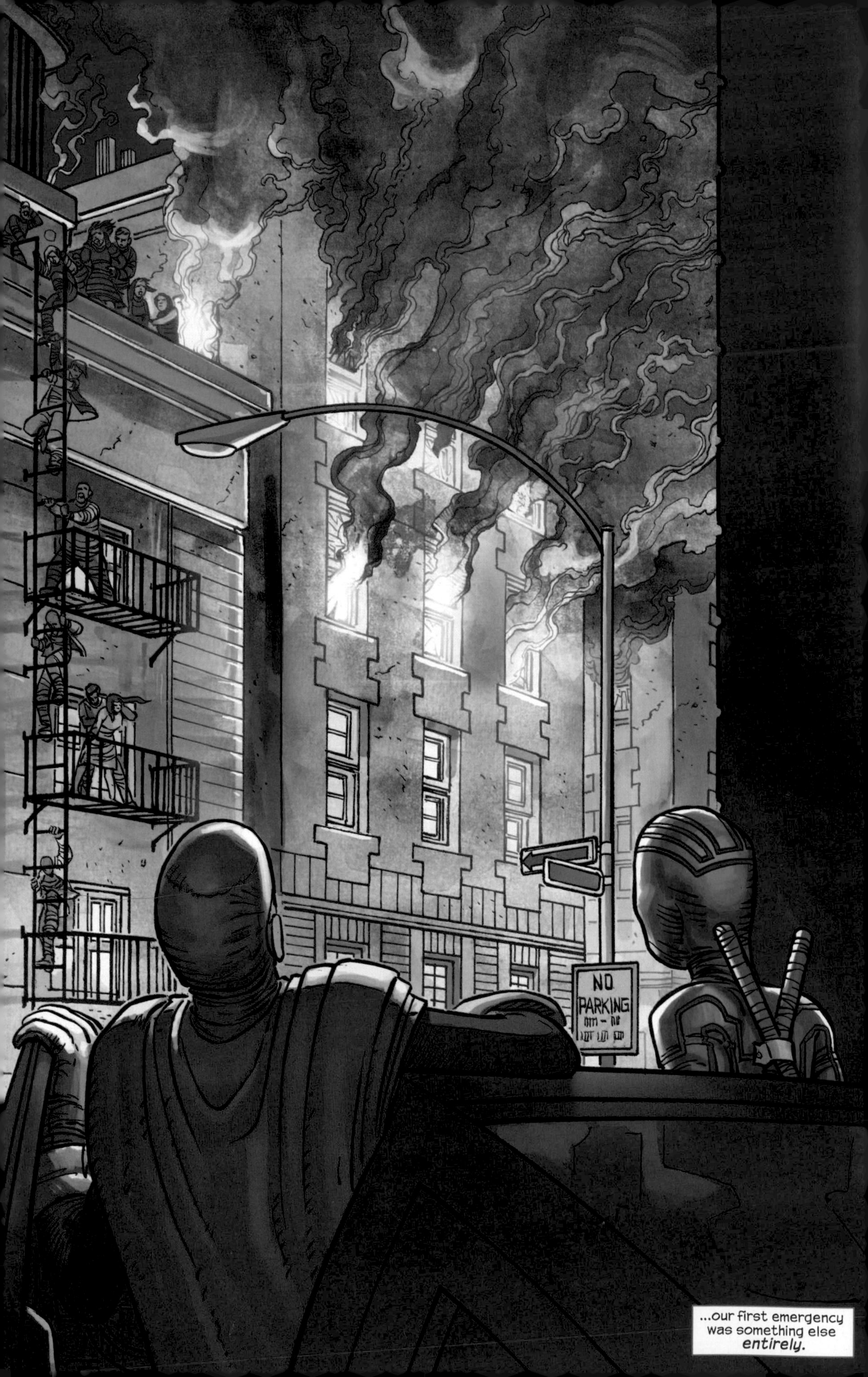
NO PARKING
...our first emergency was something else *entirely.*

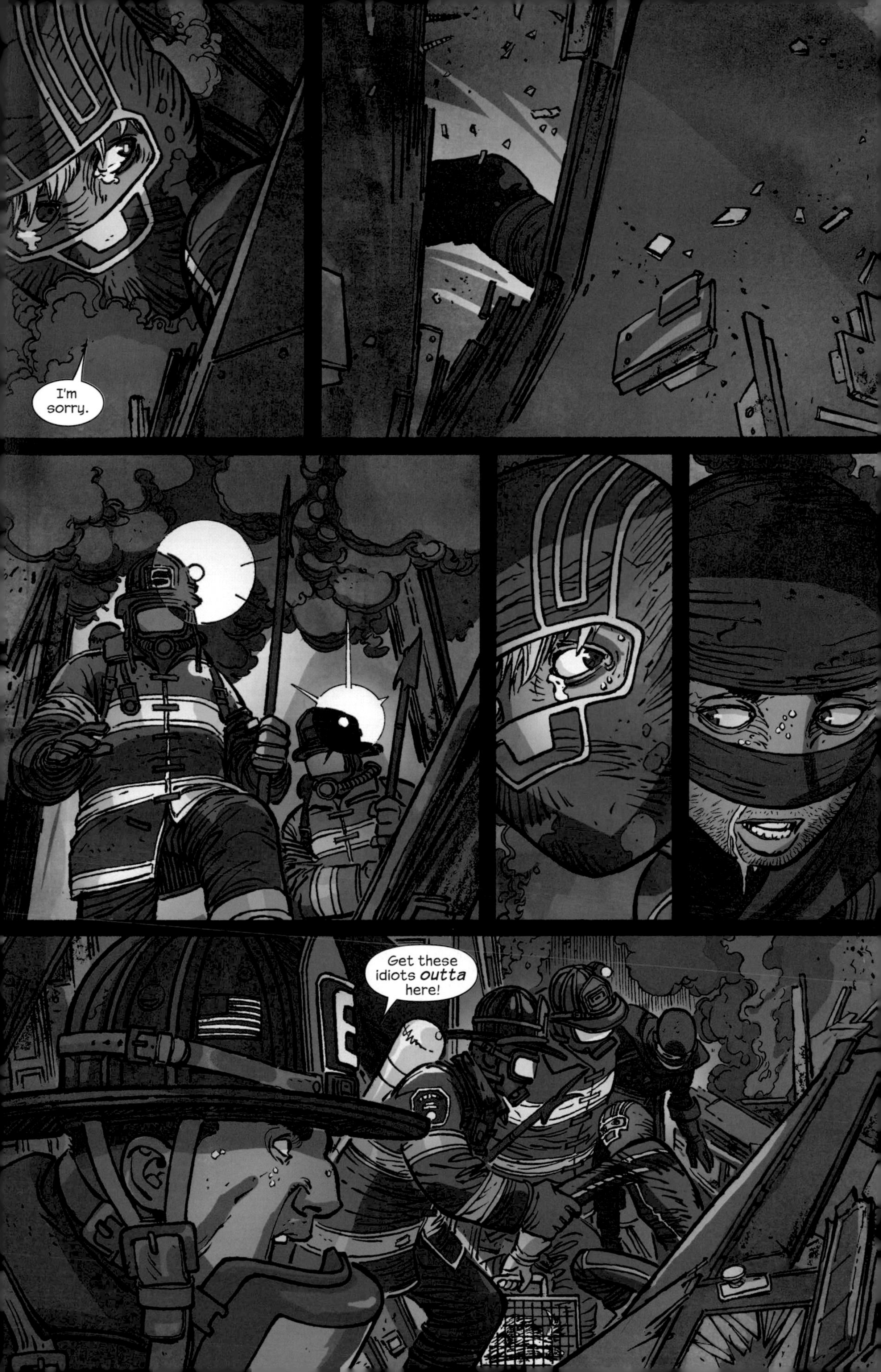
I'm sorry.
Get these idiots outta here!

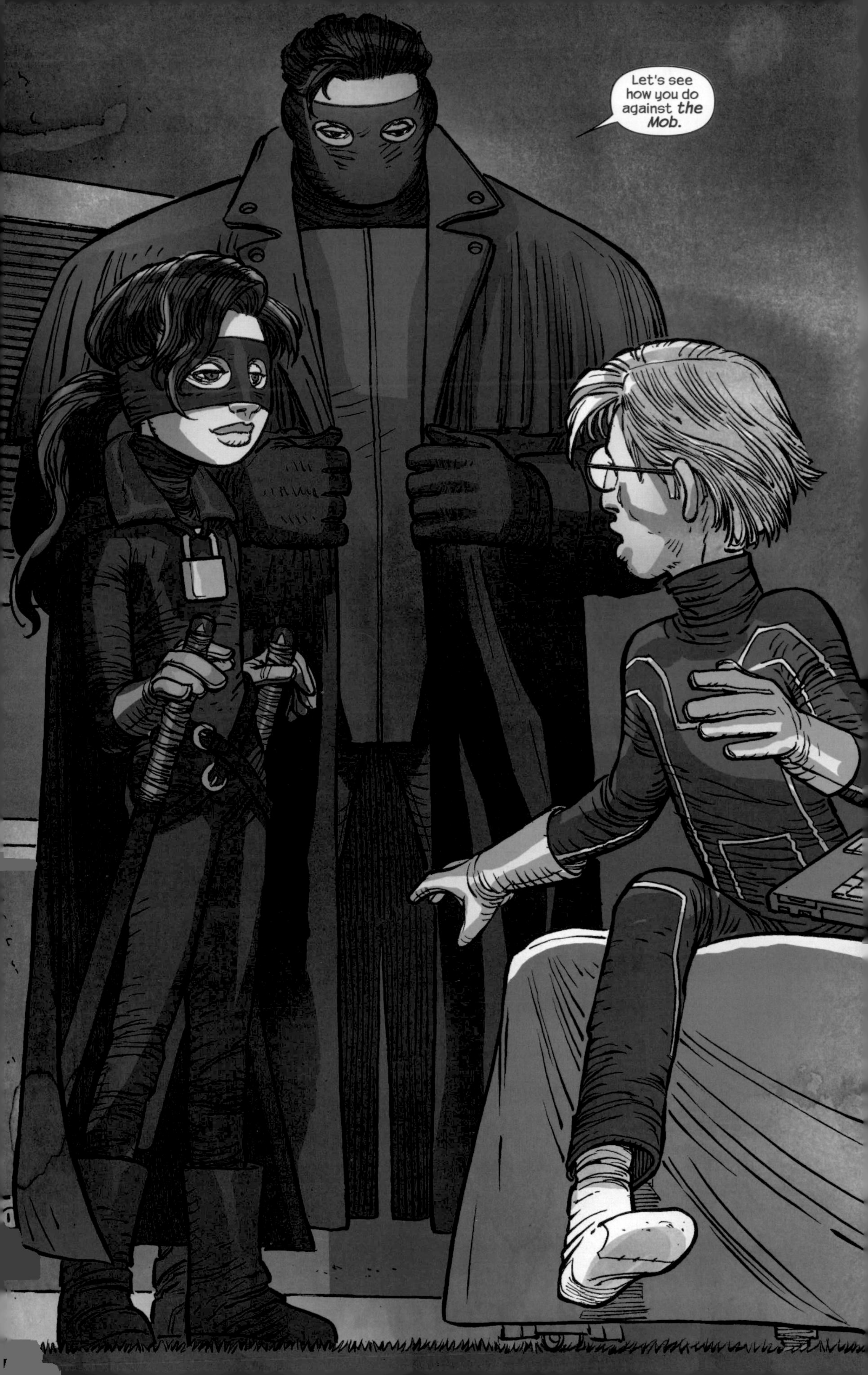
Let's see how you do against *the Mob.*

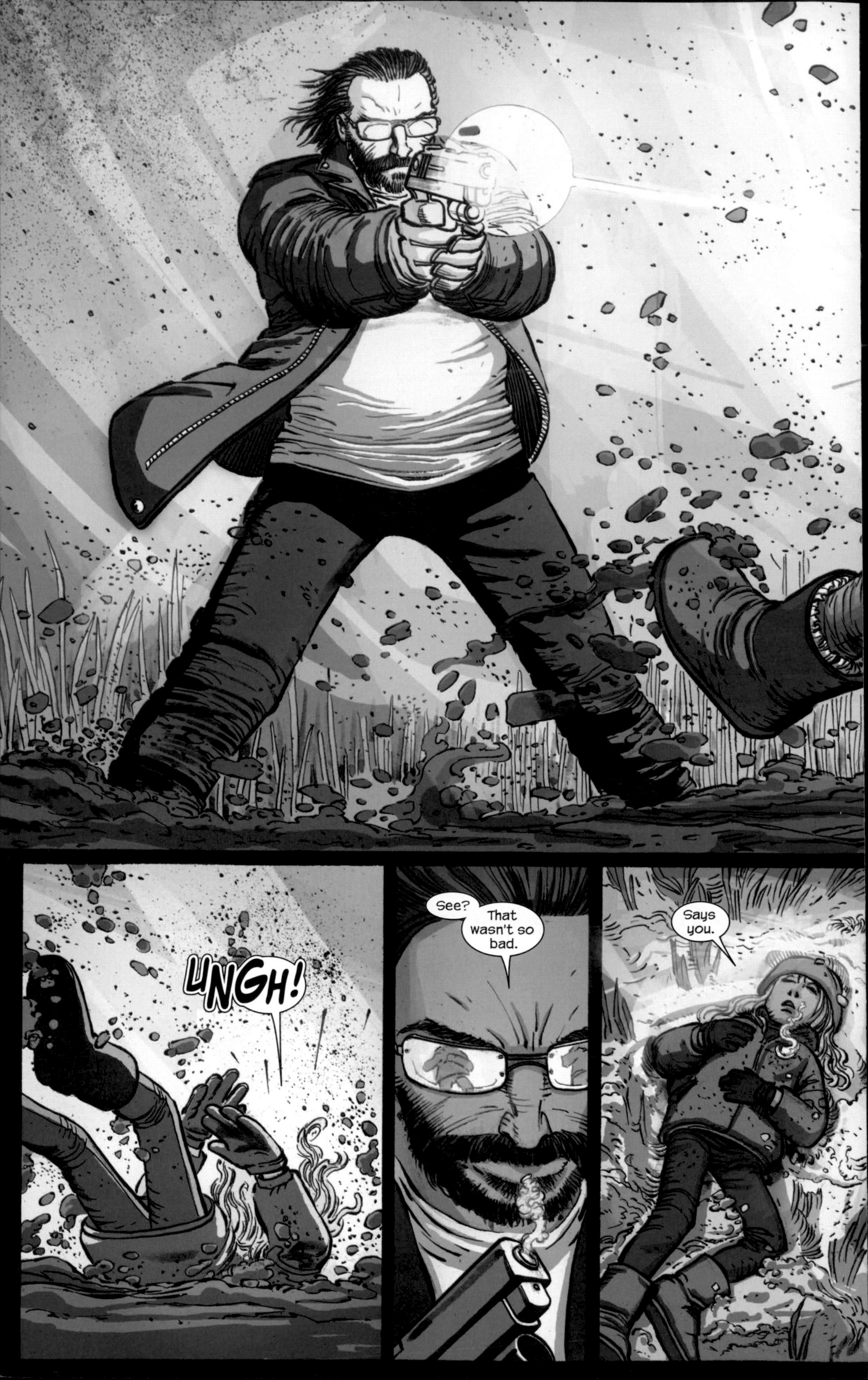
UNGH!
See?
That wasn't so bad.
Says you.

Aw, the Kevlar's crying more than *you* are, baby. Besides, now you know what it feels like, you won't be scared when some scrawny junkie *asshole* pulls a forty-five.

What do we do when a junkie pulls a forty-five?

Knife in the nuts?

Good girl.

Now dust yourself down and we'll do another *ten rounds.*

Then, if you're good and I'm feeling extra-generous, we'll go get ourselves an *ice-cream sundae.*

Cool.

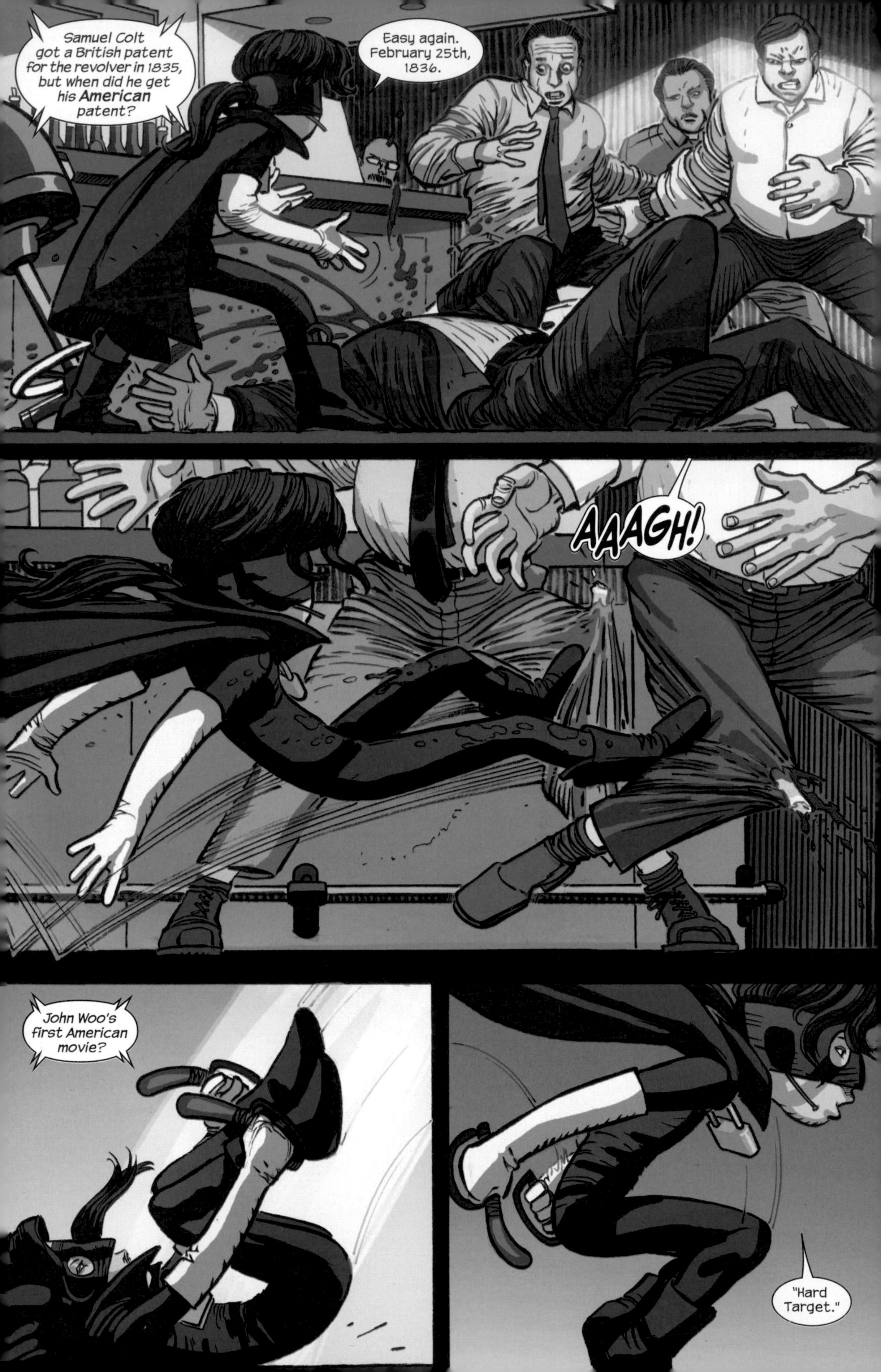
Samuel Colt got a British patent for the revolver in 1835, but when did he get his **American** patent?
Easy again. February 25th, 1836.
AAAGH!
John Woo's first American movie?
"Hard Target."

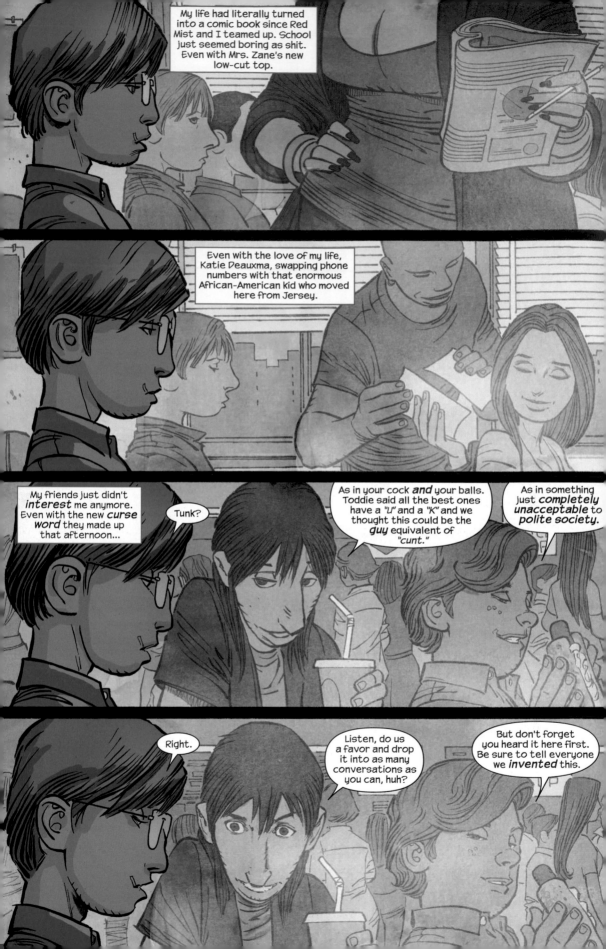

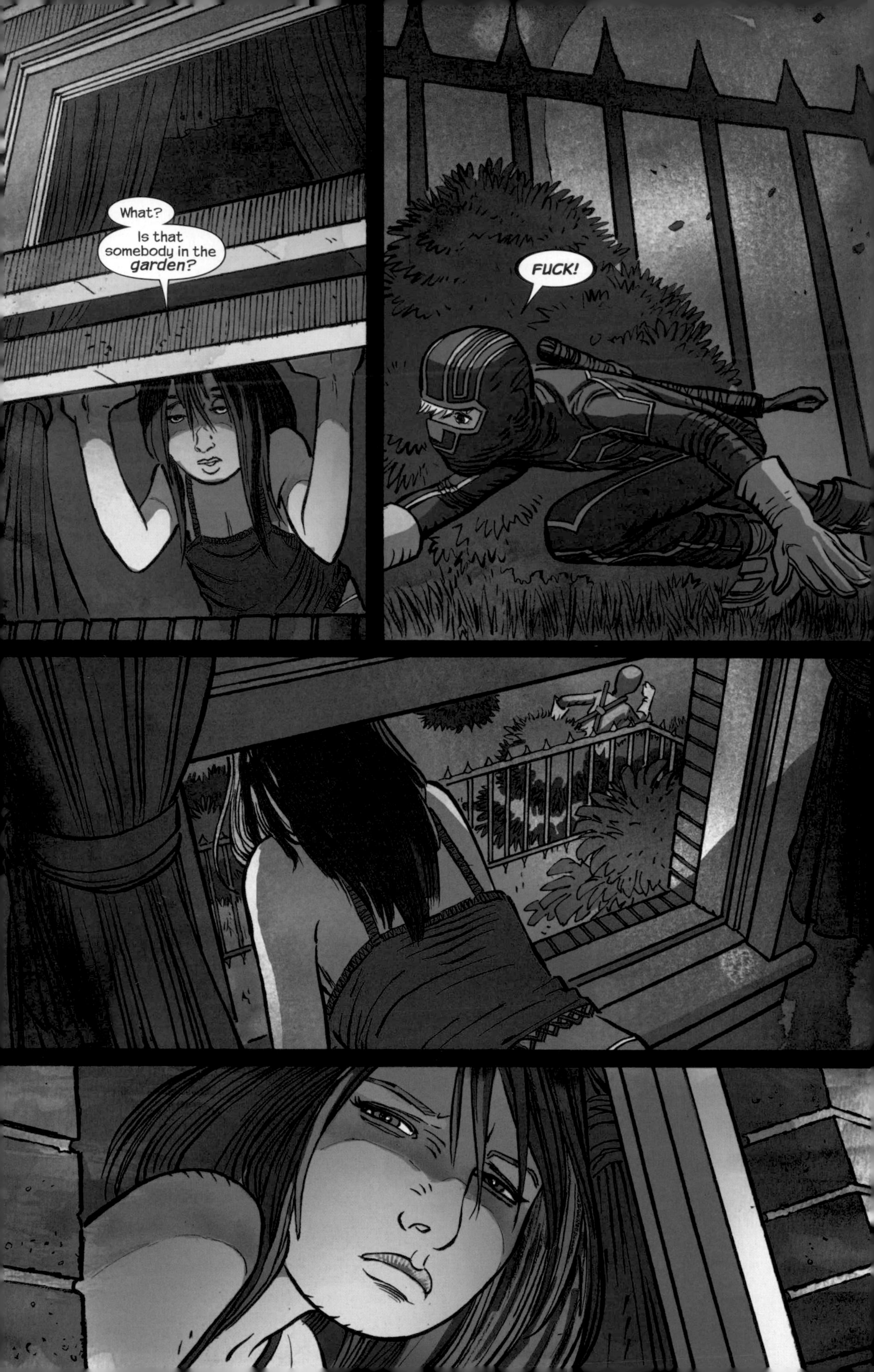
What?
Is that somebody in the garden?
FUCK!

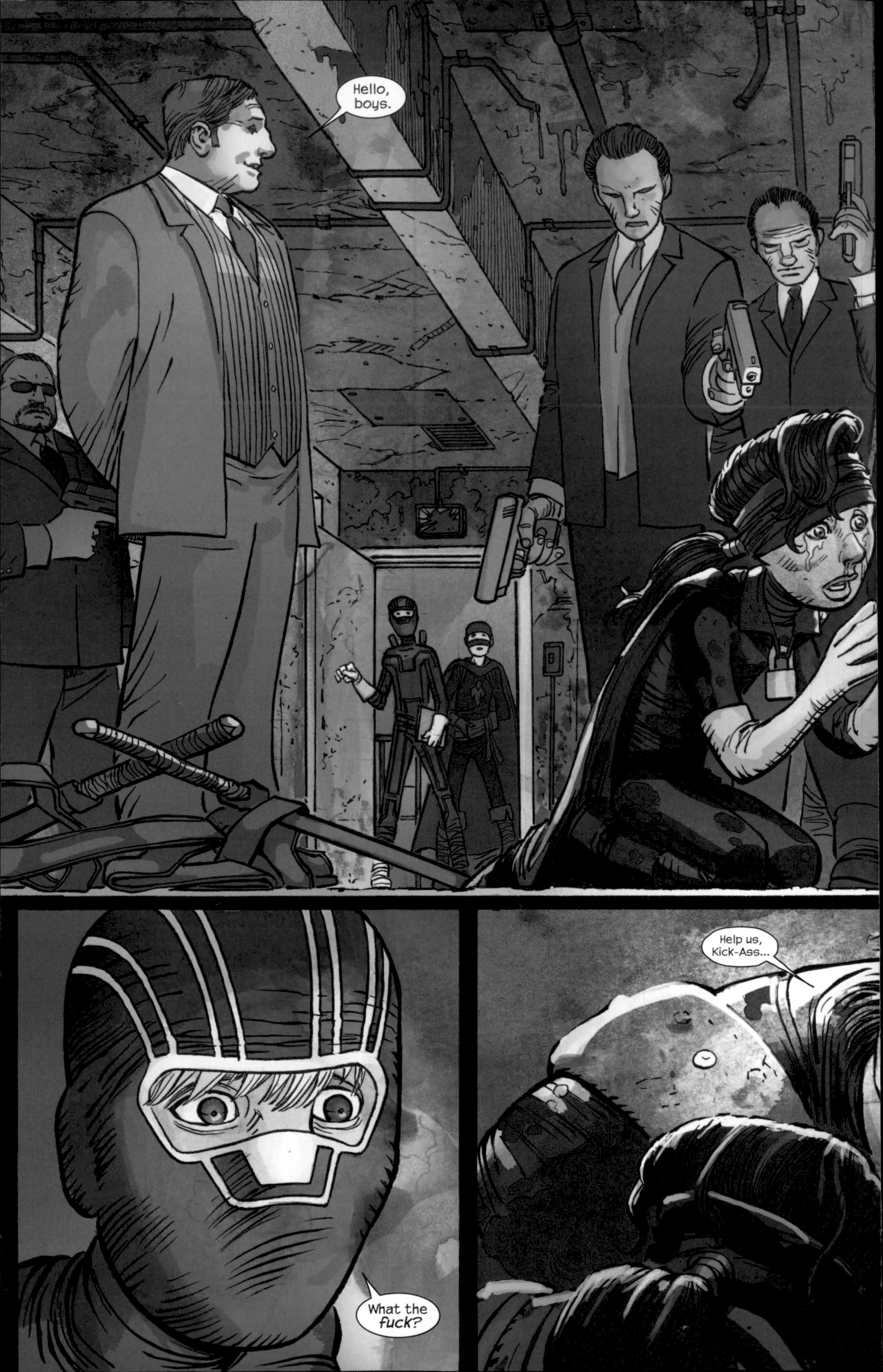
Hello, boys.
What the fuck?
Help us, Kick-Ass...

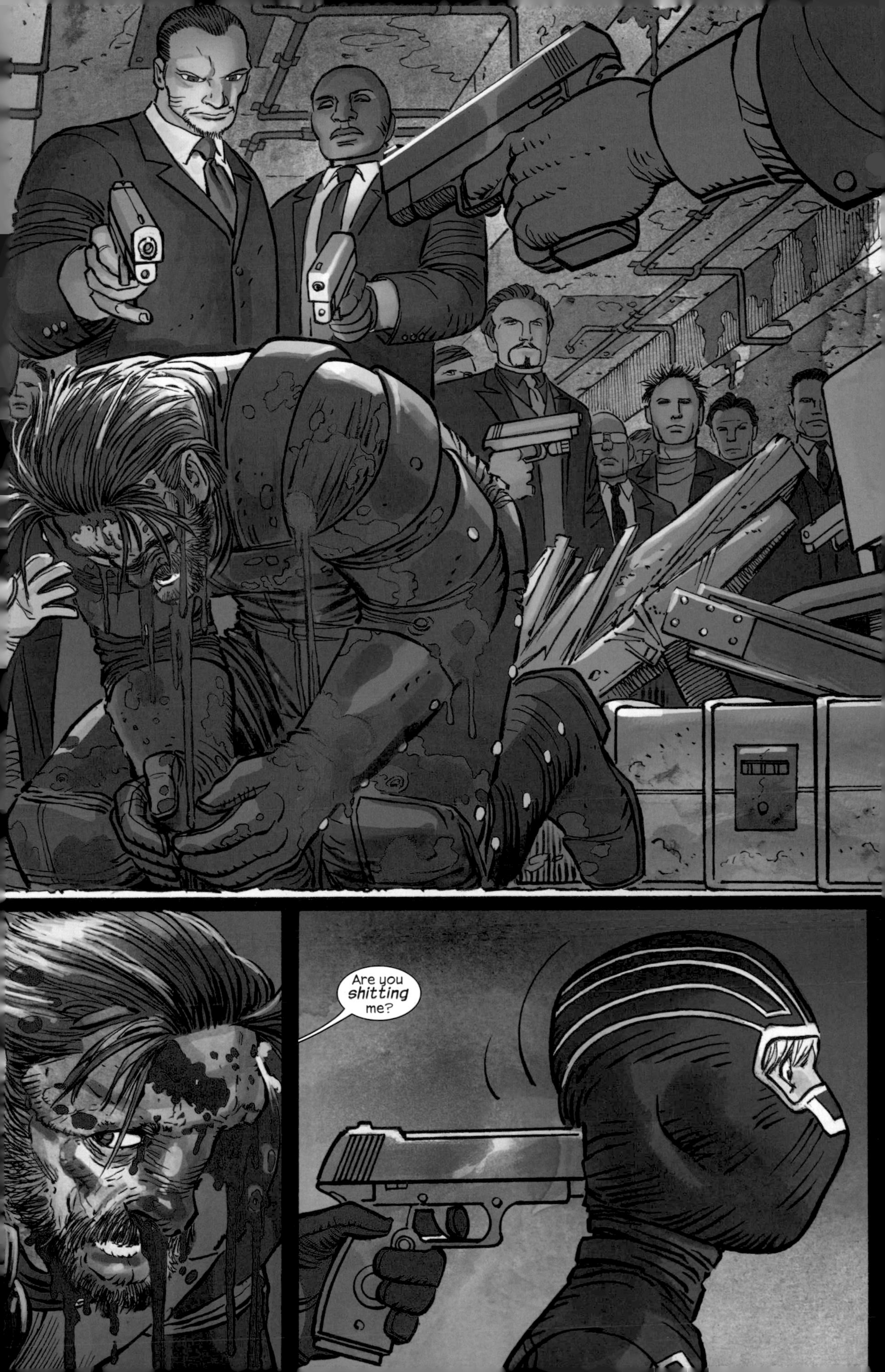
Are you shitting me?

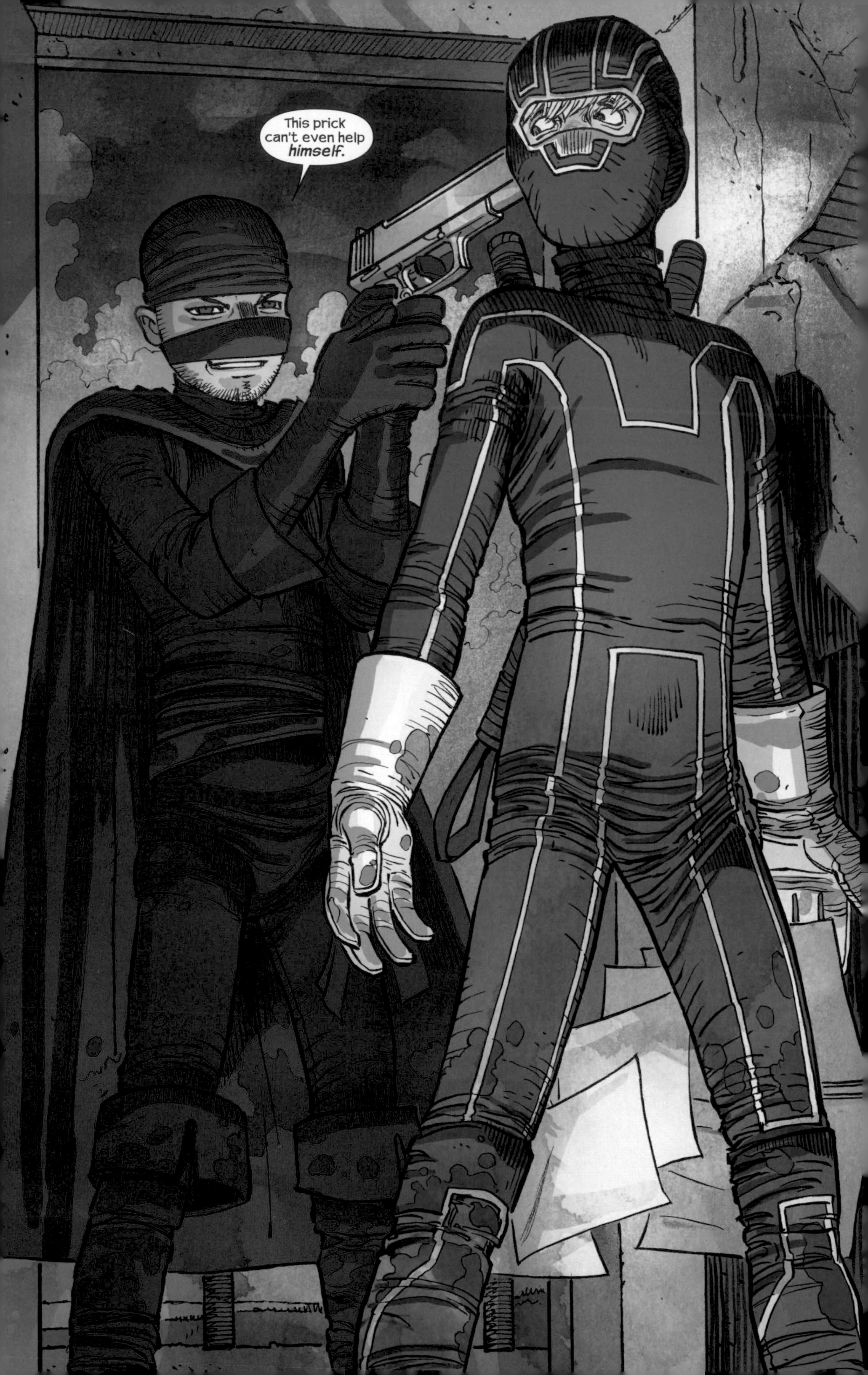
This prick can't even help *himself*.

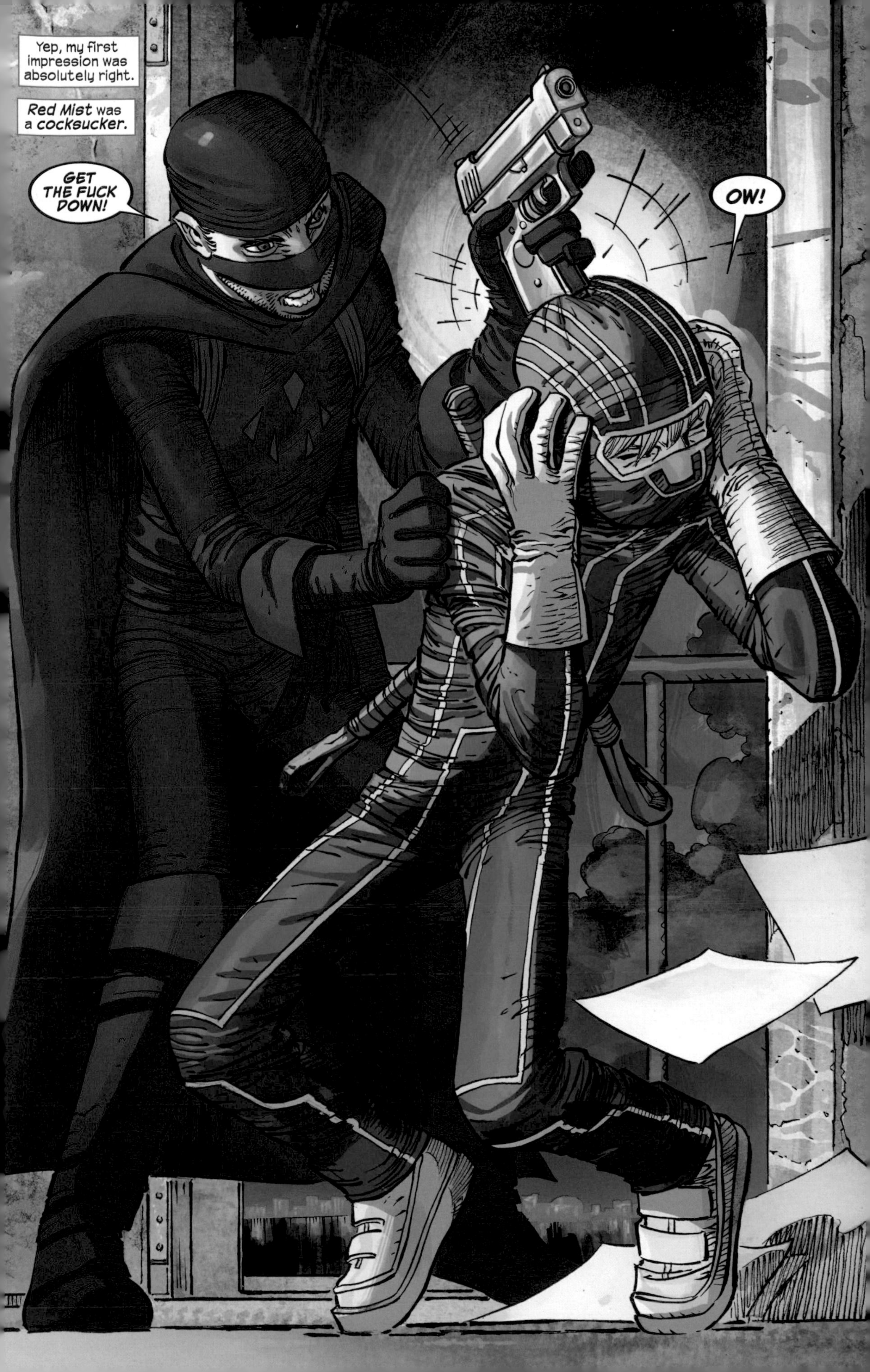
Yep, my first impression was absolutely right.
Red Mist was a cocksucker.
GET THE FUCK DOWN!
OW!

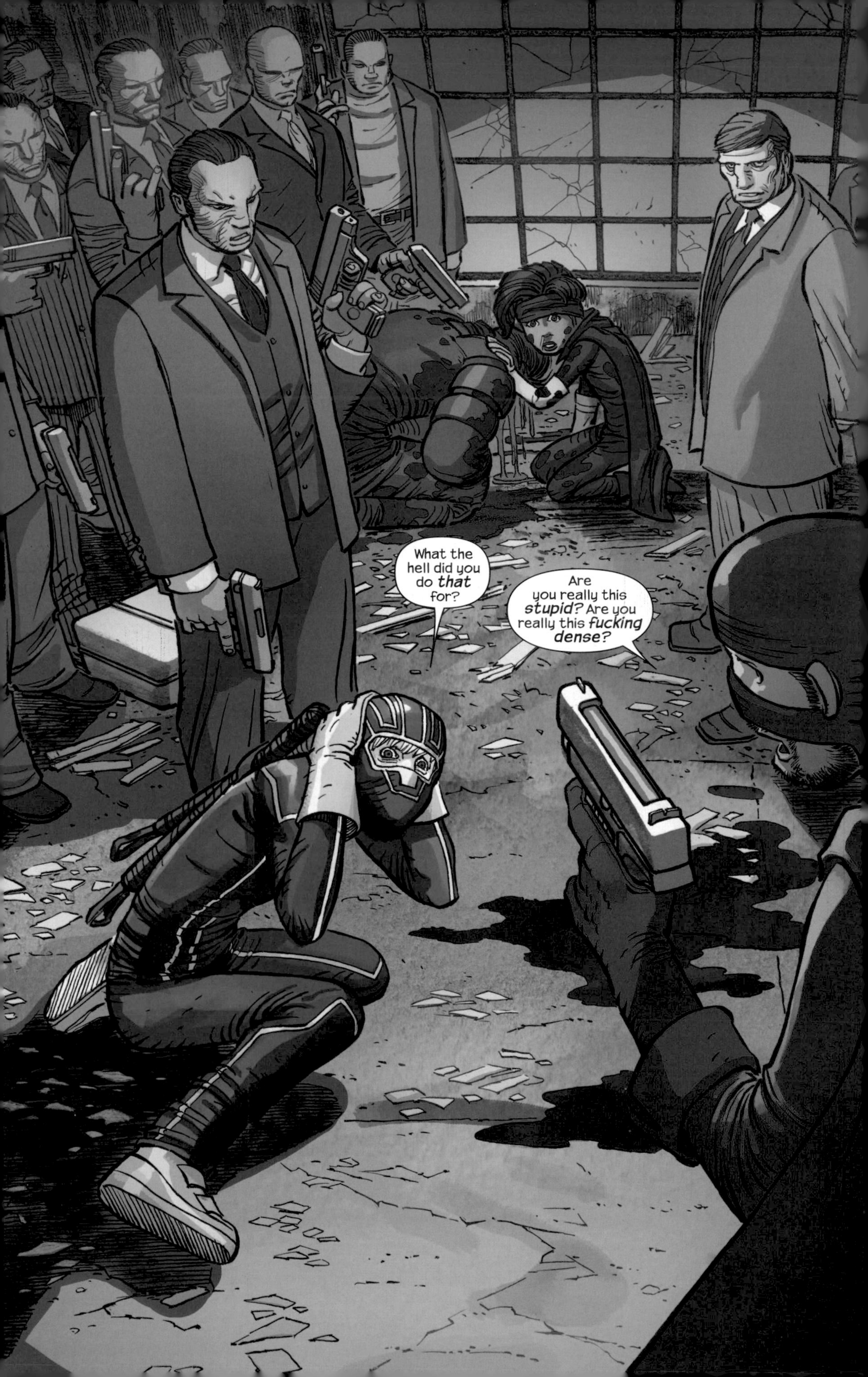
What the hell did you do *that* for?
Are you really this *stupid*? Are you really this *fucking dense*?

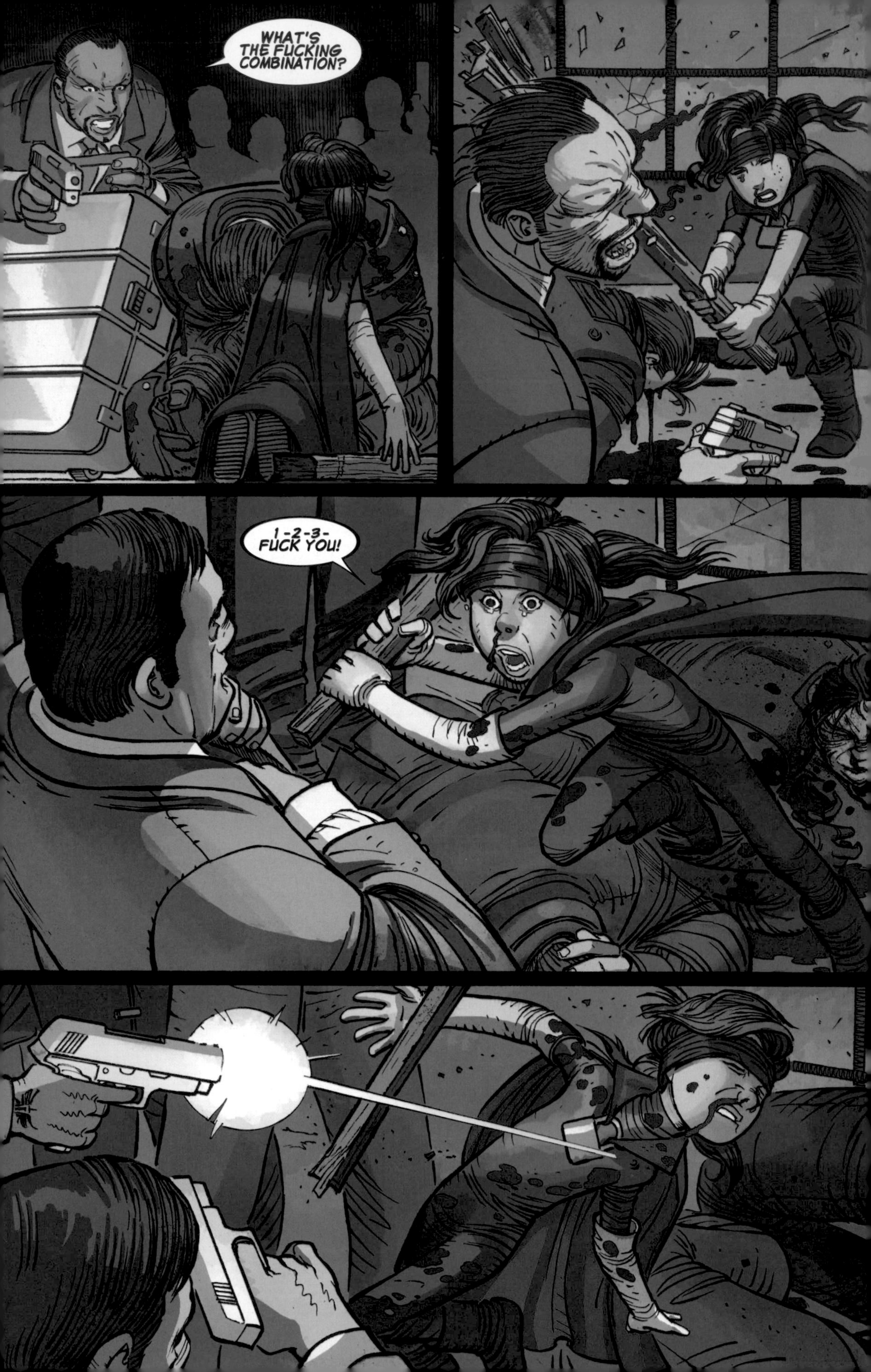
WHAT'S THE FUCKING COMBINATION?
1-2-3- FUCK YOU!

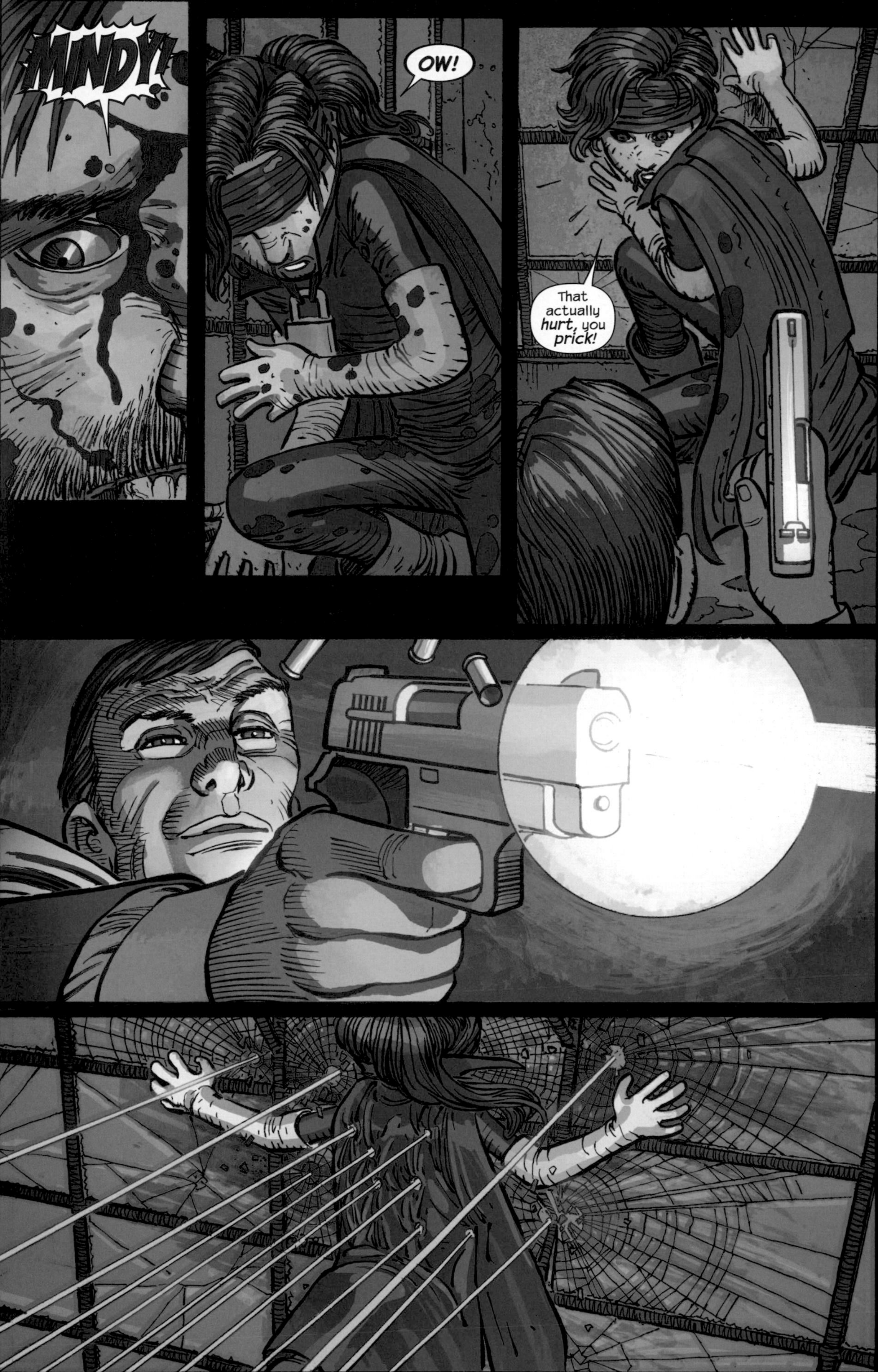
MINDY!
OW!
That actually *hurt*, you *prick!*

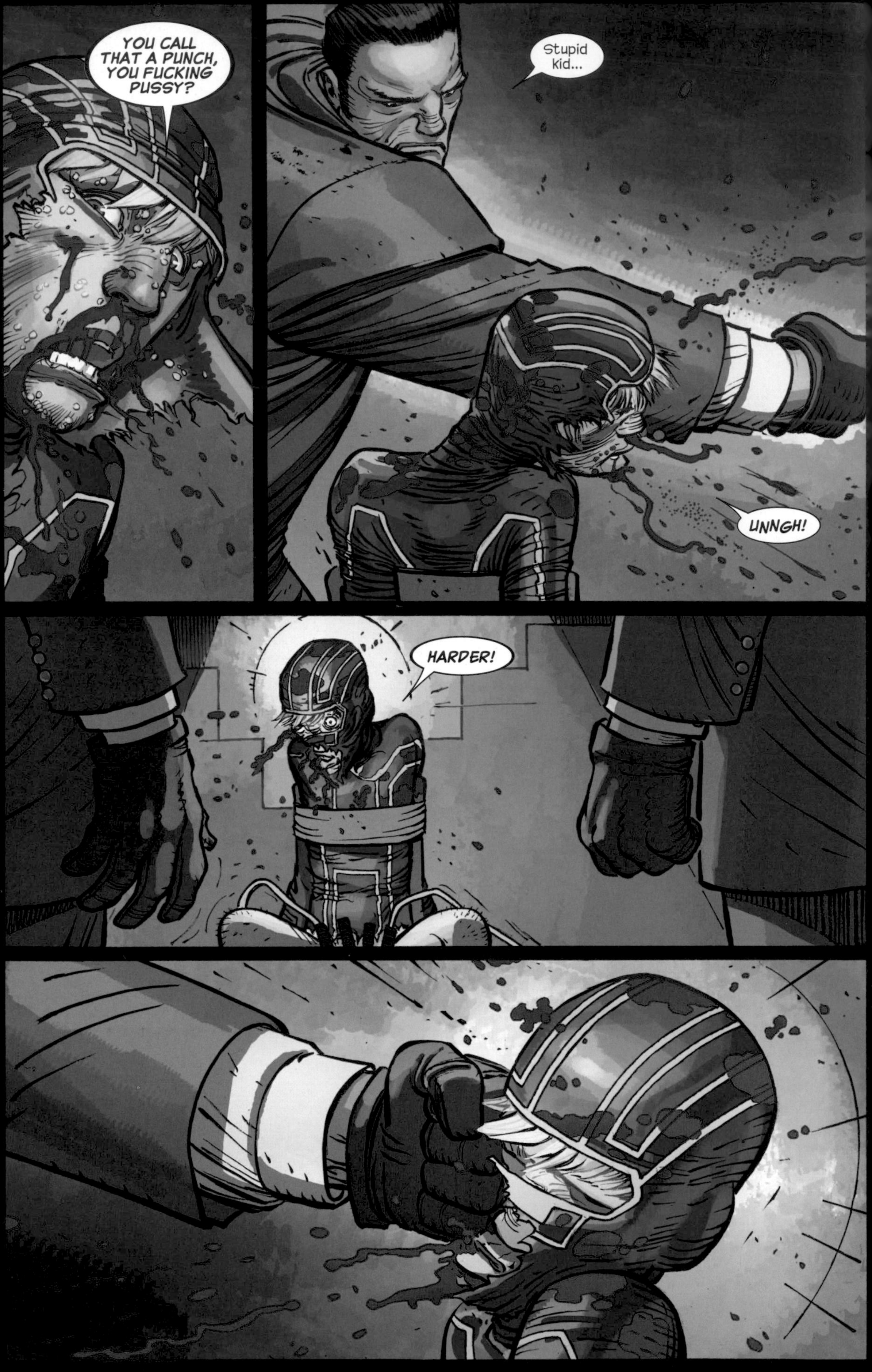
YOU CALL THAT A PUNCH, YOU FUCKING PUSSY?
Stupid kid...
UNNGH!
HARDER!

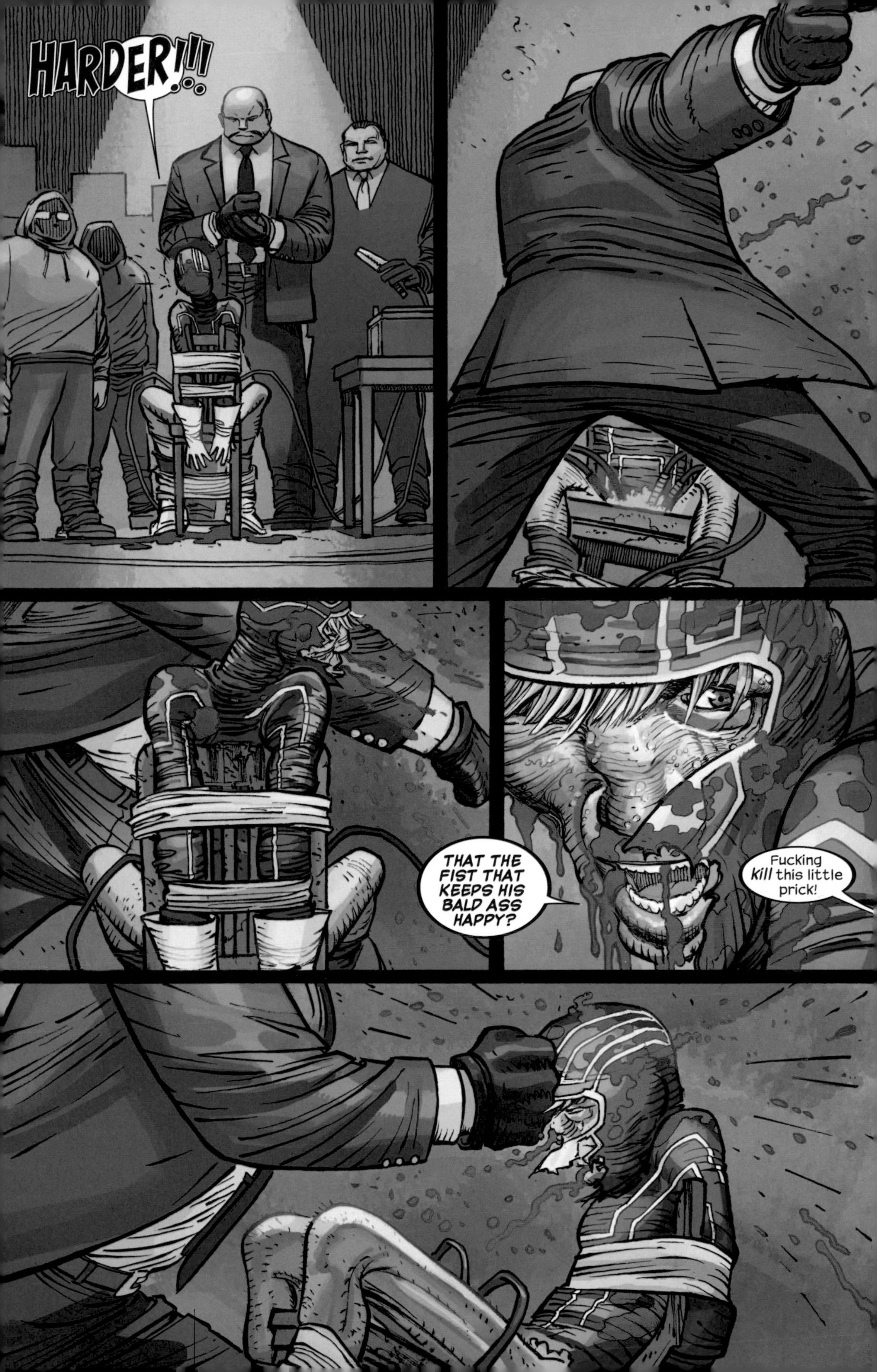
HARDER!!!
THAT THE FIST THAT KEEPS HIS BALD ASS HAPPY?
Fucking *kill* this little prick!

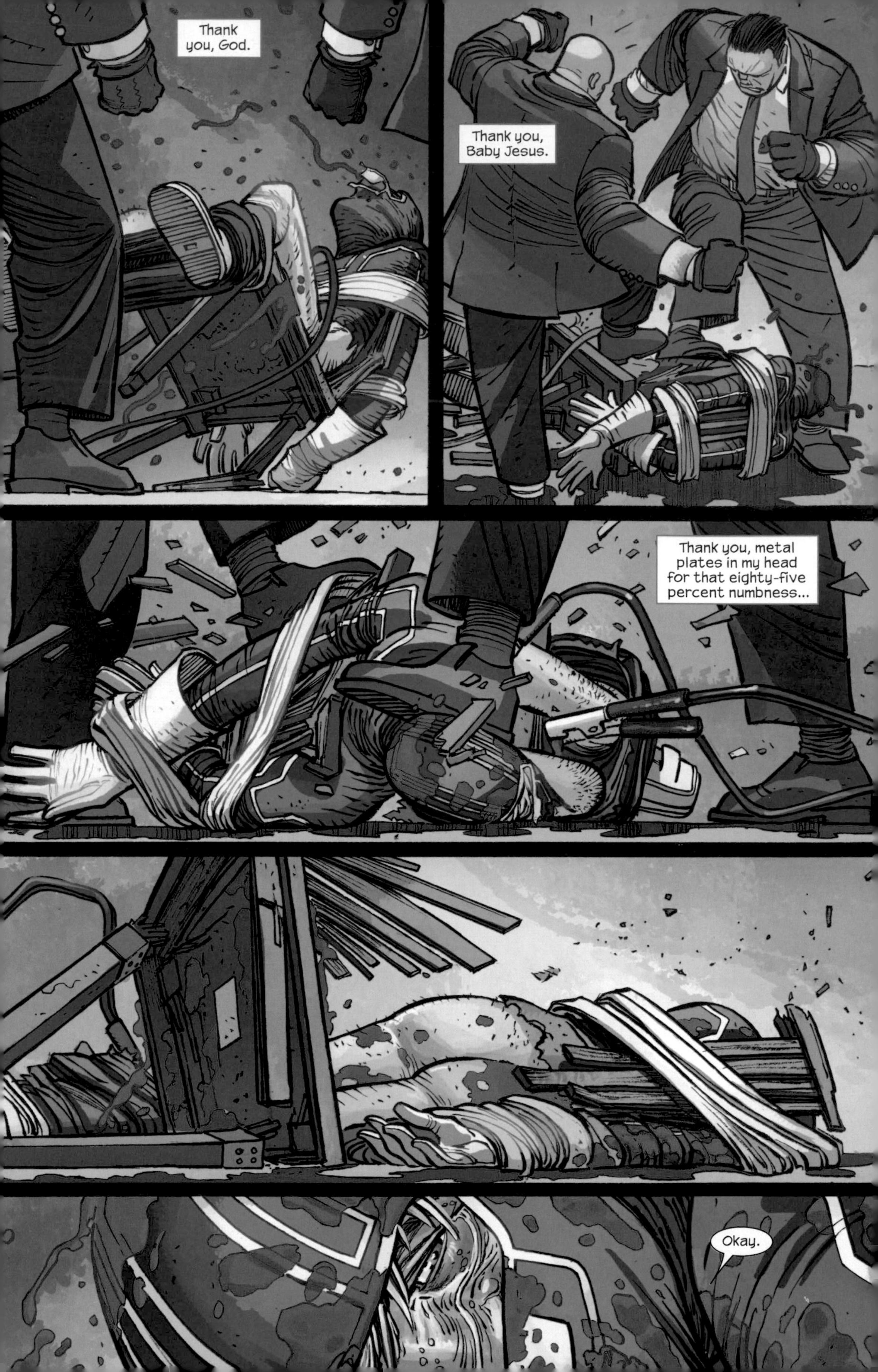
Thank you, God.
Thank you, Baby Jesus.
Thank you, metal plates in my head for that eighty-five percent numbness...
Okay.

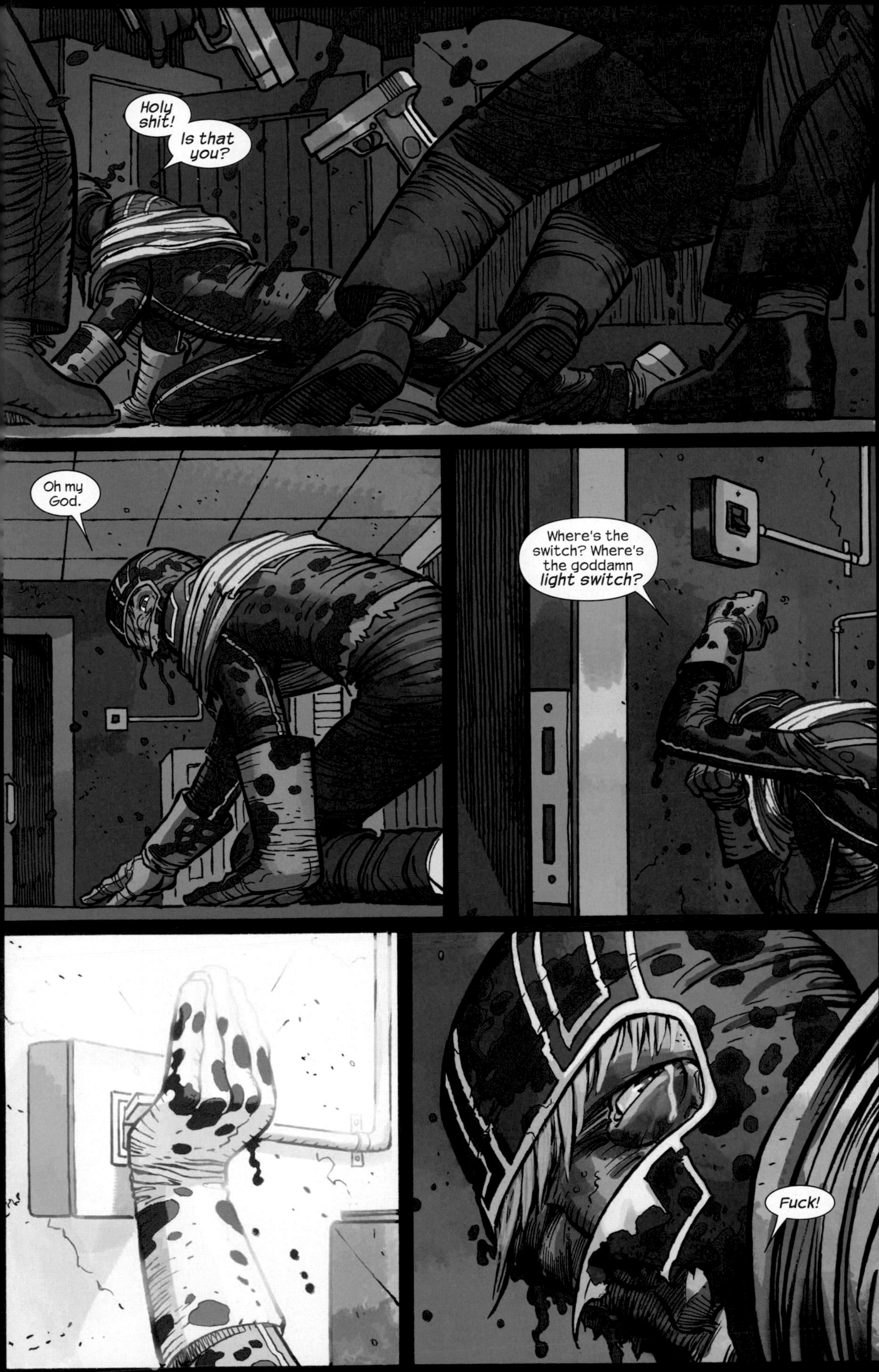

Holy shit!
Is that you?
Oh my God.
Where's the switch? Where's the goddamn *light switch?*
Fuck!

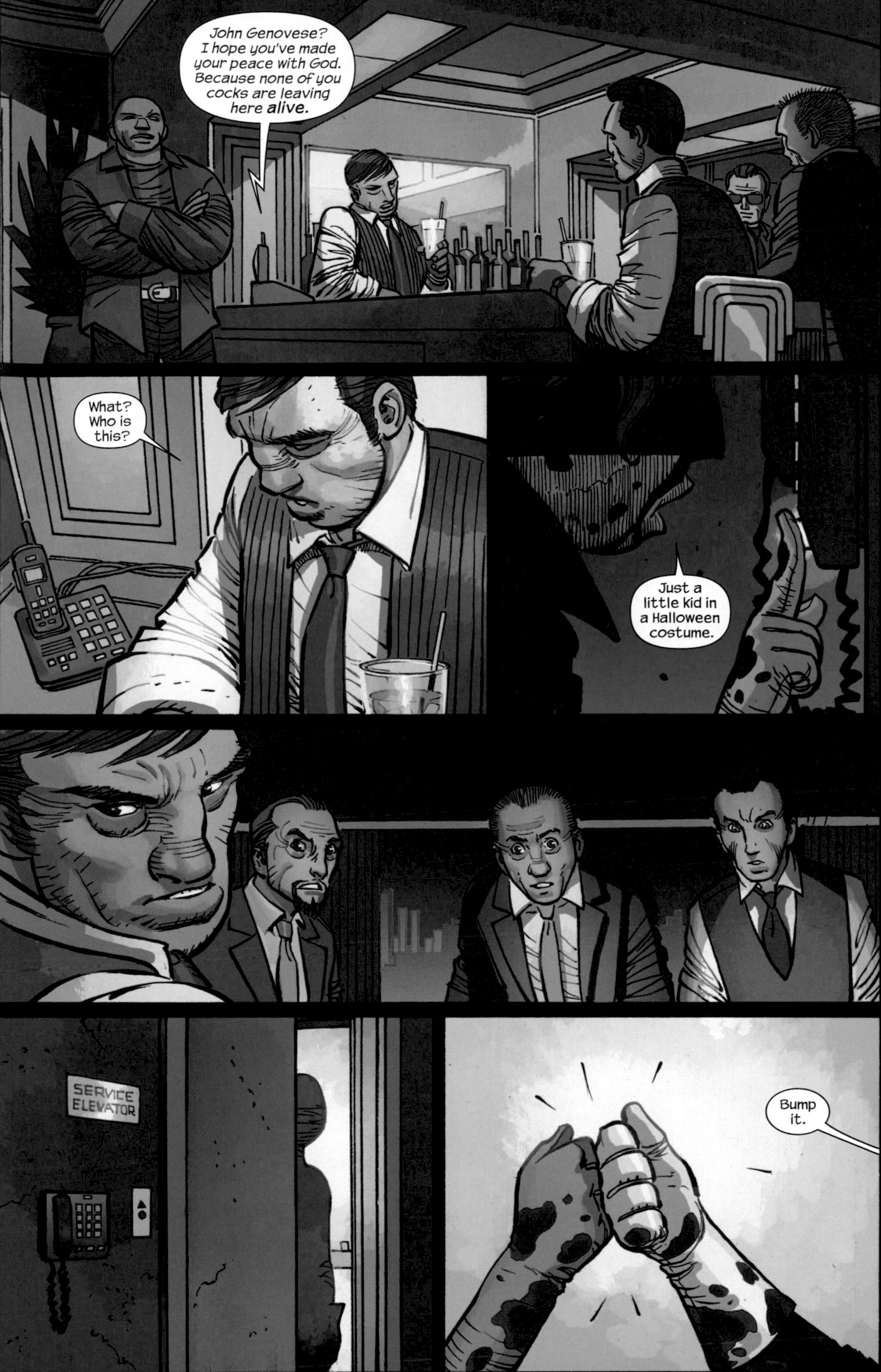

John Genovese? I hope you've made your peace with God. Because none of you cocks are leaving here alive.
What? Who is this?
Just a little kid in a Halloween costume.
SERVICE ELEVATOR
Bump it.

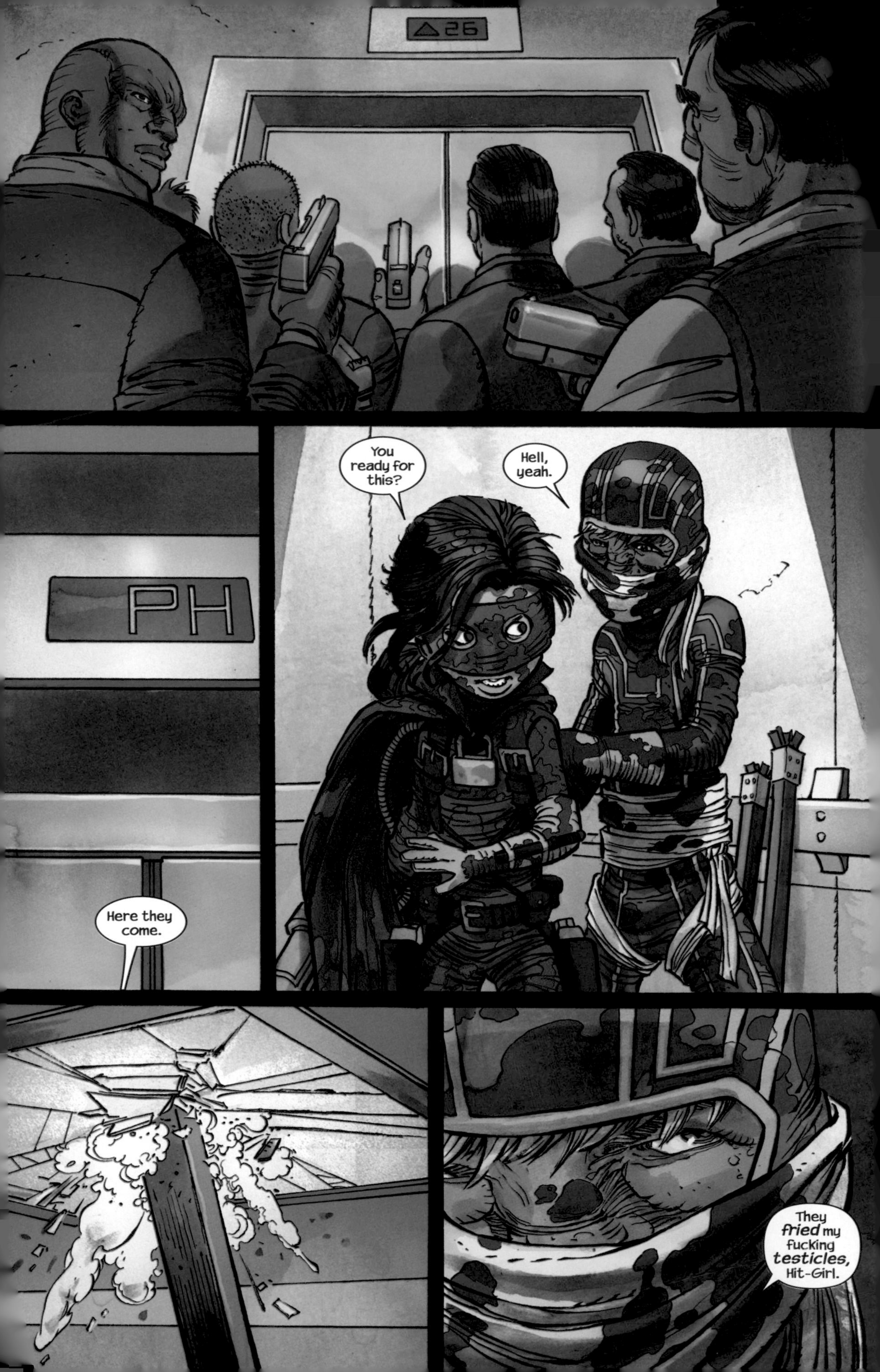

26
PH
Here they come.
You ready for this?
Hell, yeah.
They *fried* my fucking *testicles*, Hit-Girl.

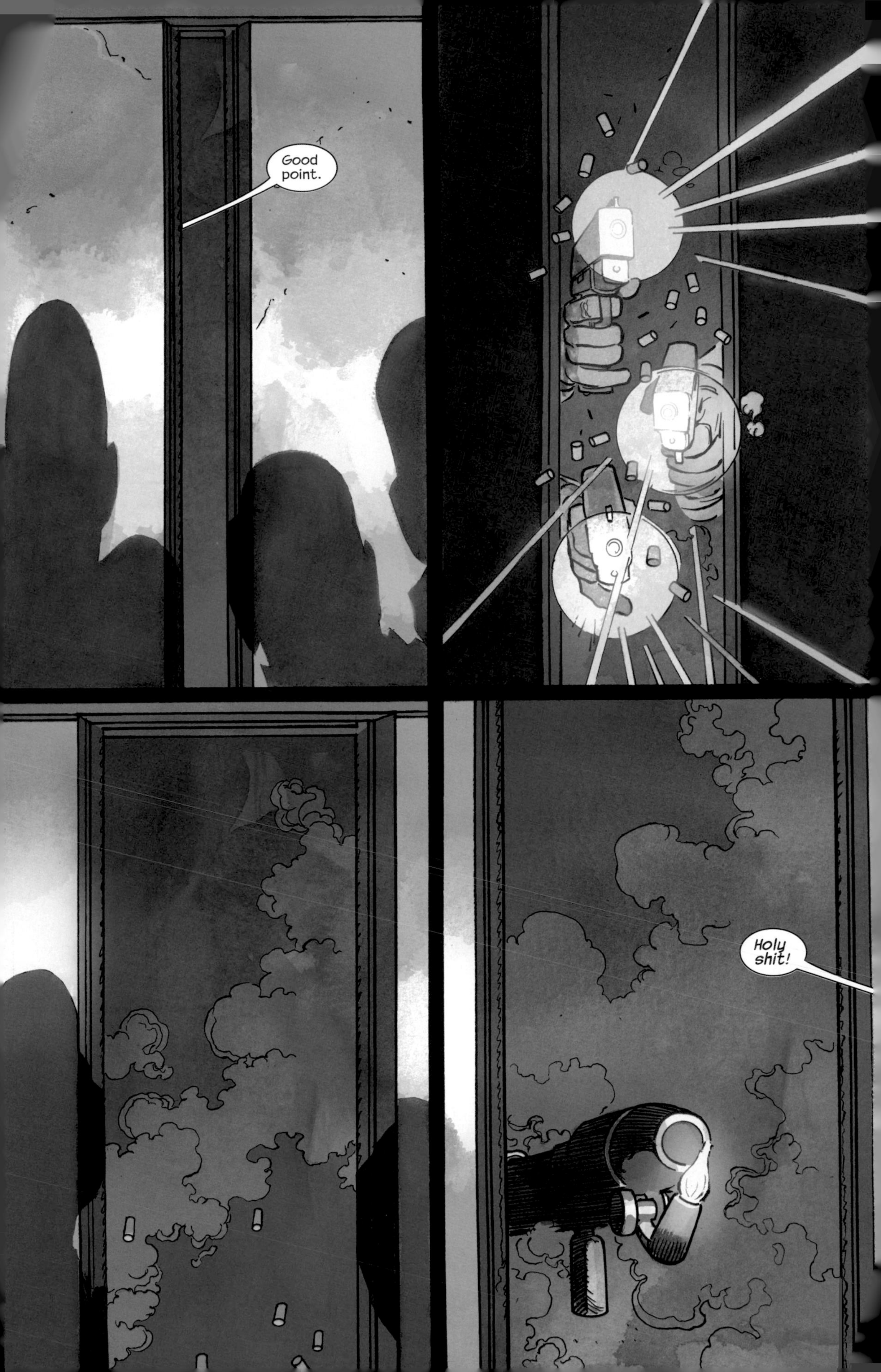
Good point.
Holy shit!

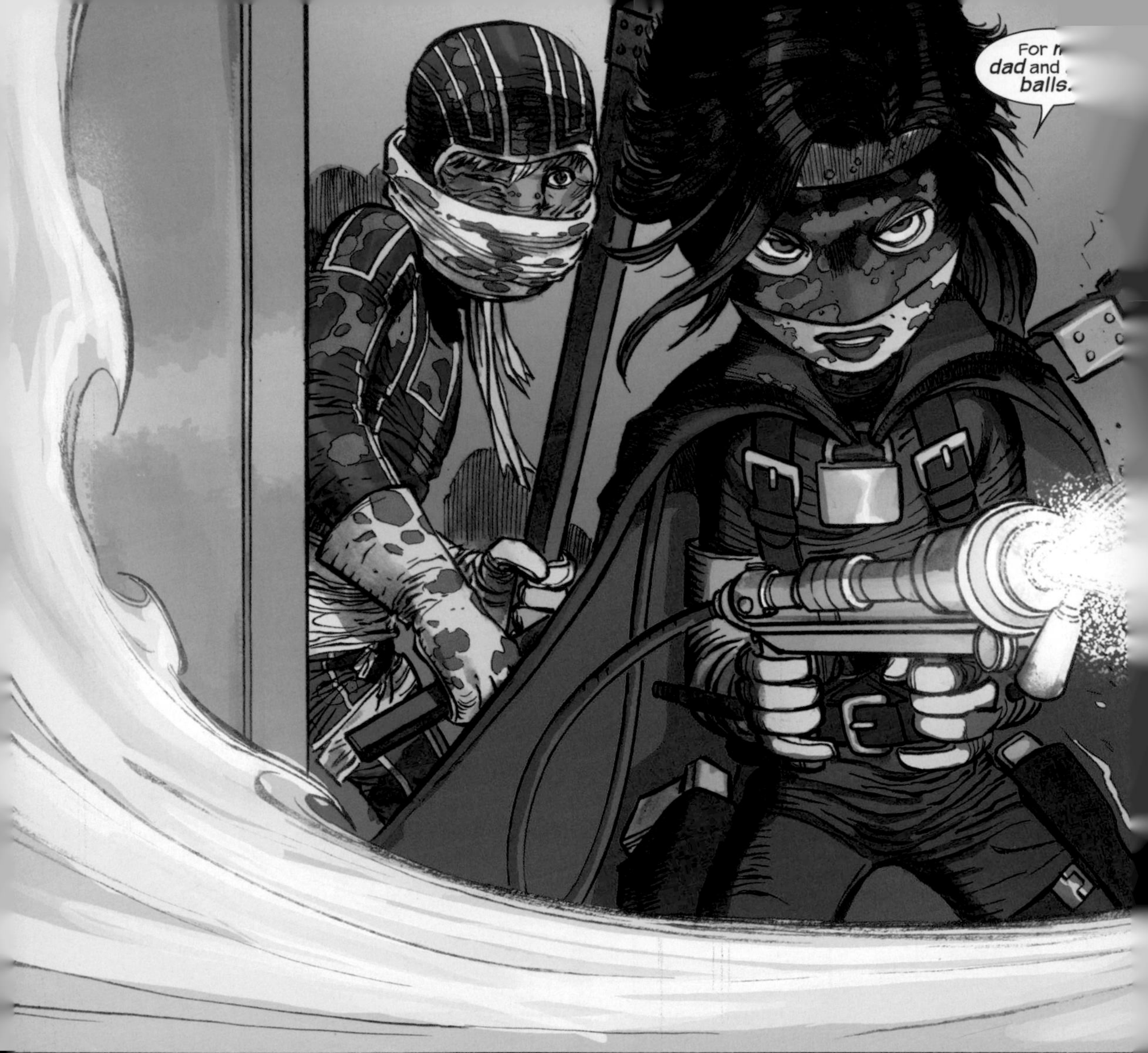
For m
dad and
balls.

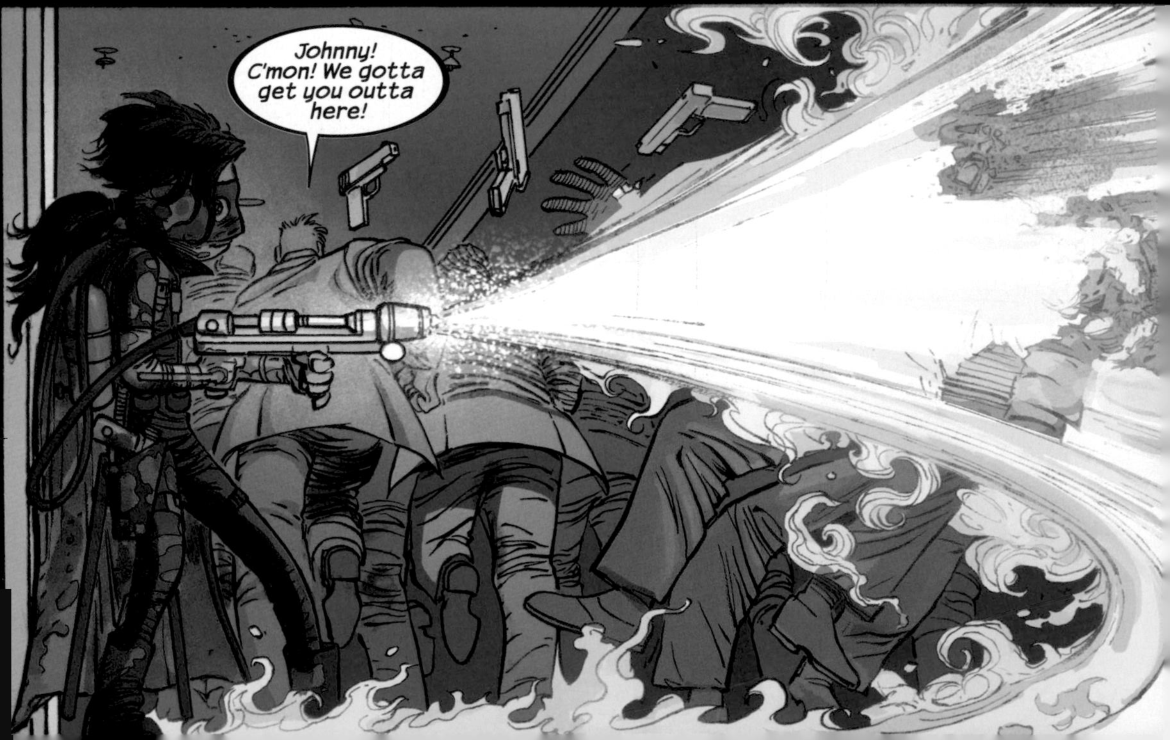
Johnny! C'mon! We gotta get you outta here!

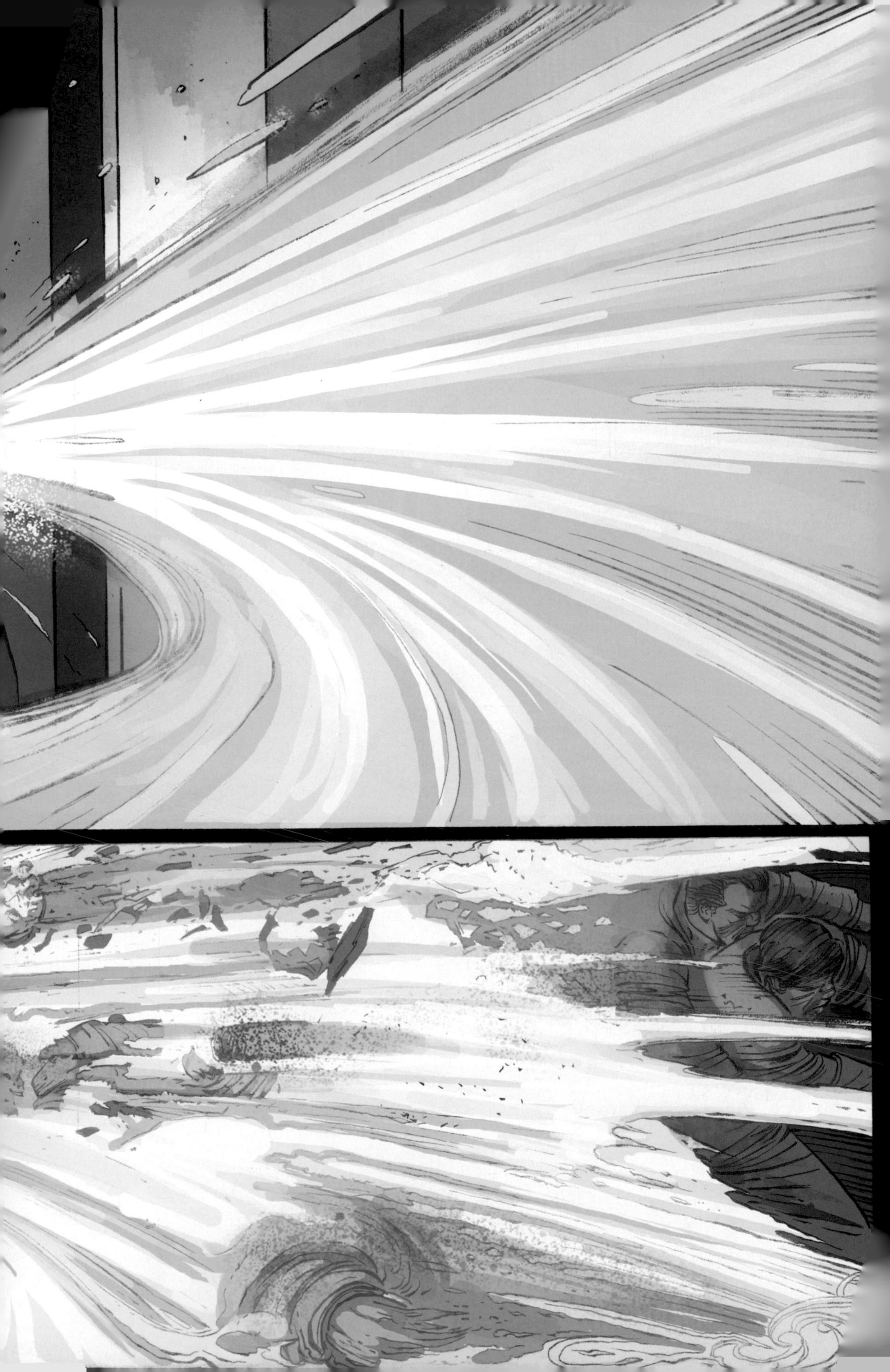

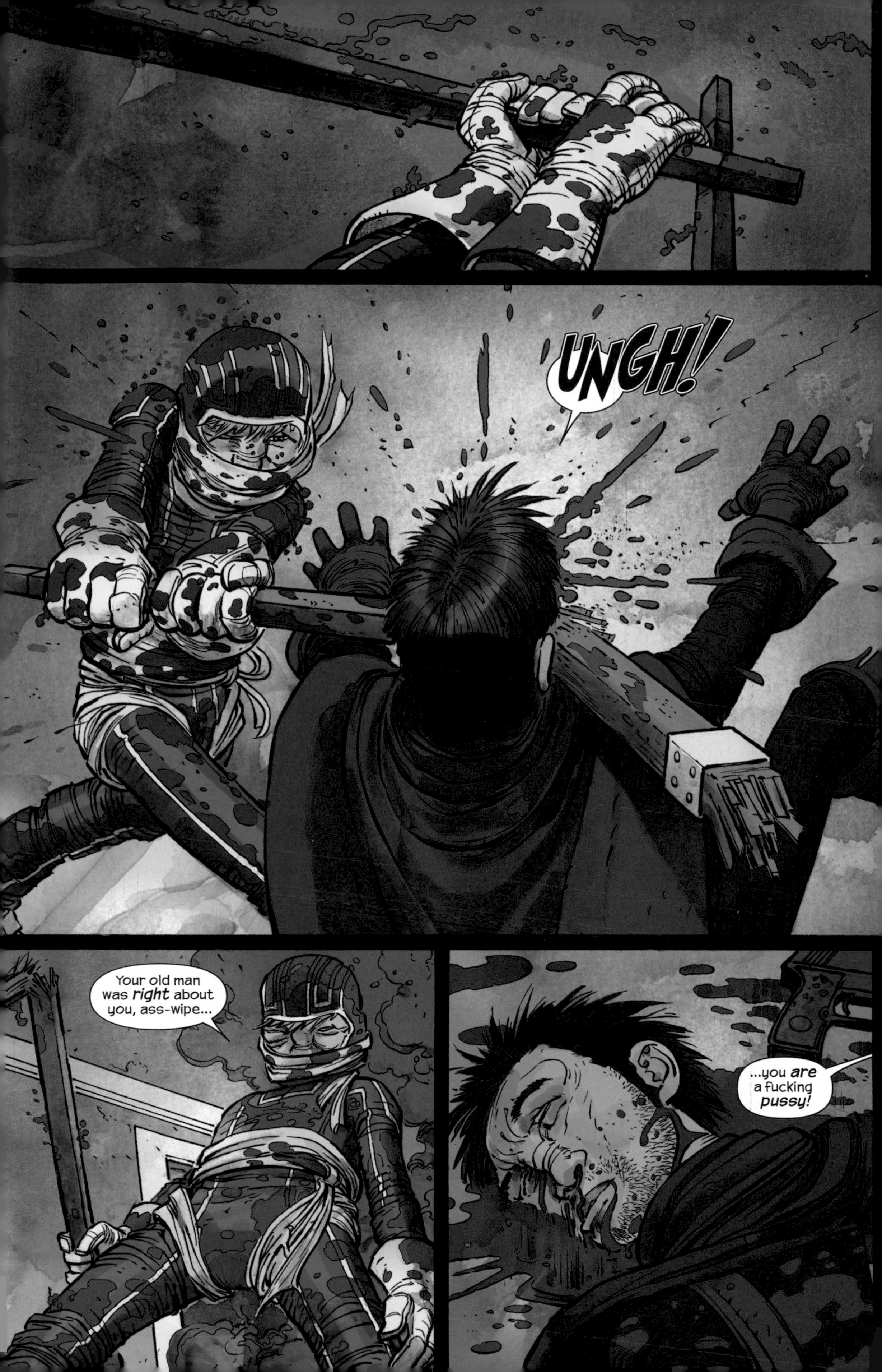
UNGH!
Your old man was right about you, ass-wipe...
...you are a fucking pussy!

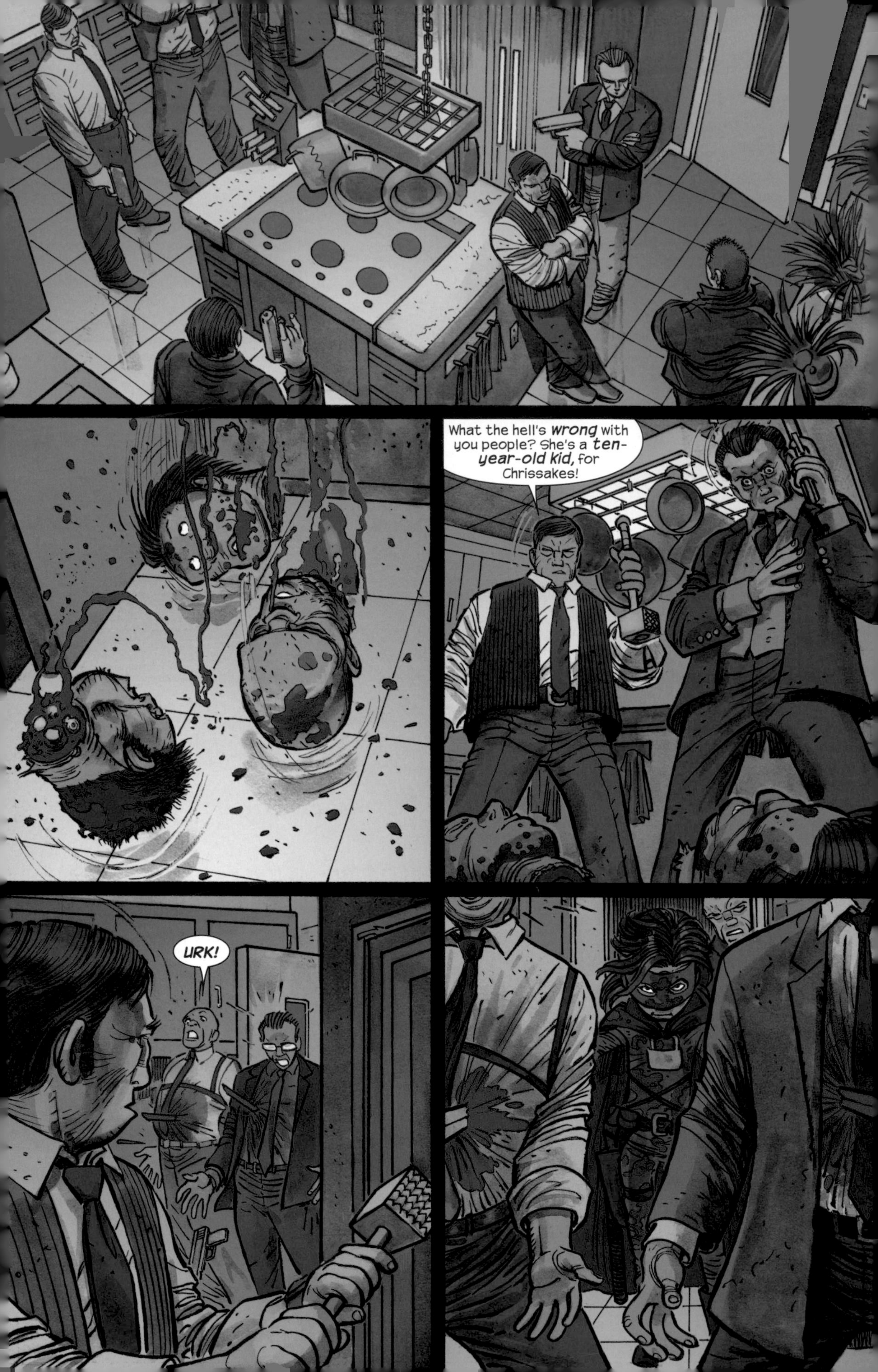
What the hell's wrong with you people? She's a ten-year-old kid, for Chrissakes!
URK!

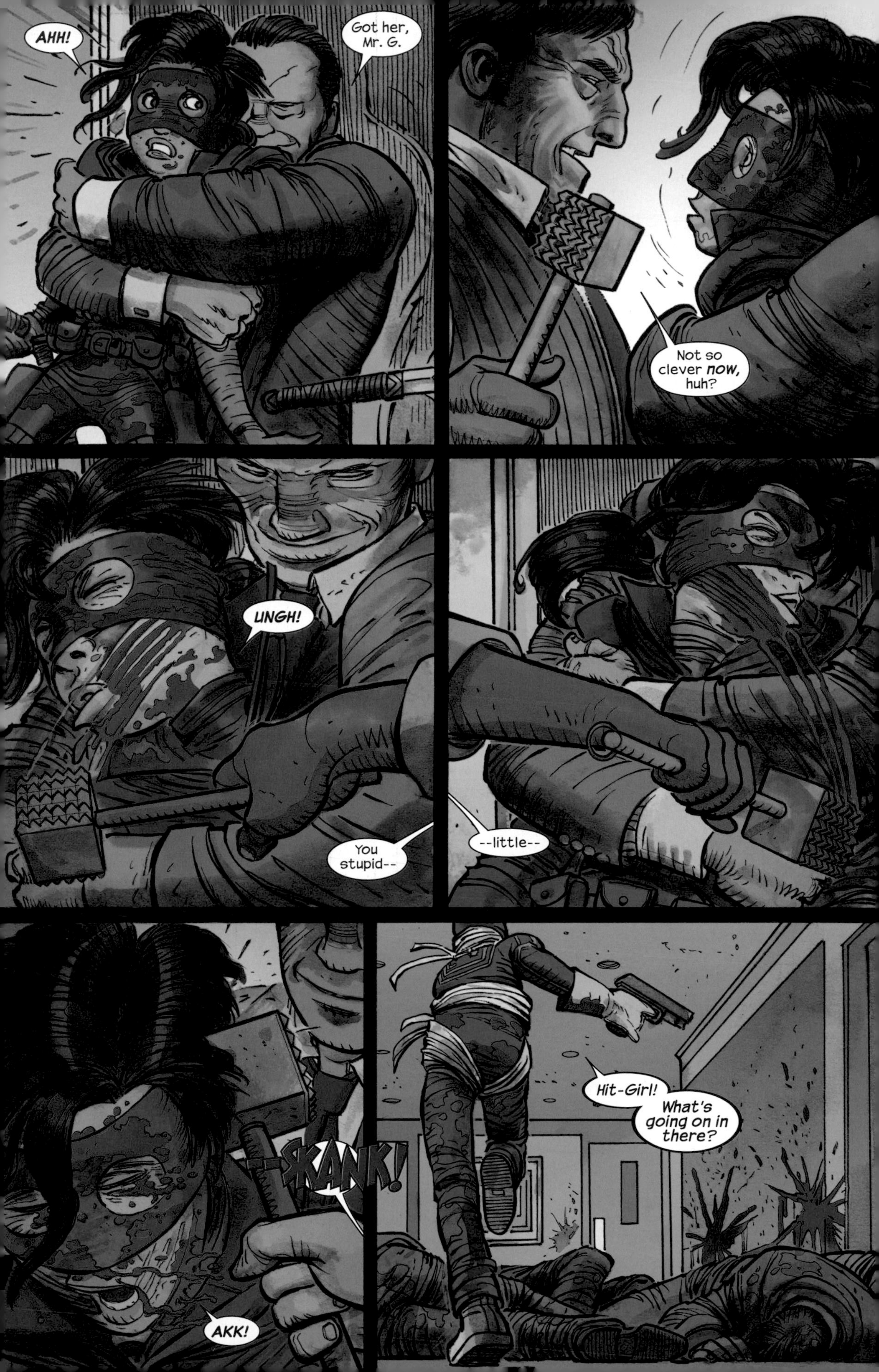
AHH!
Got her, Mr. G.
Not so clever **now,** huh?
UNGH!
You stupid--
--little--
SKANK!
AKK!
Hit-Girl! What's going on in there?

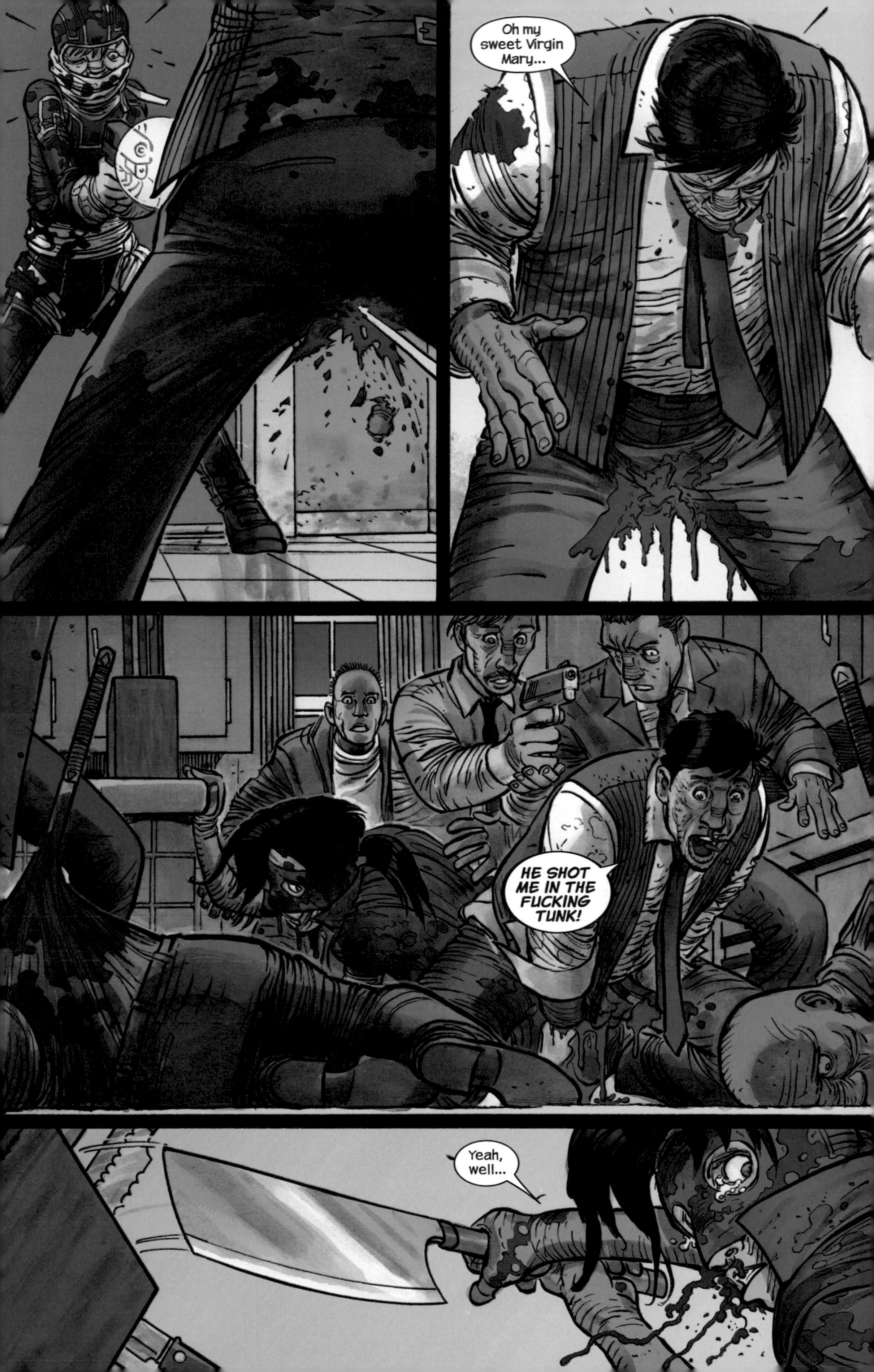
Oh my sweet Virgin Mary...
HE SHOT ME IN THE FUCKING TUNK!
Yeah, well...

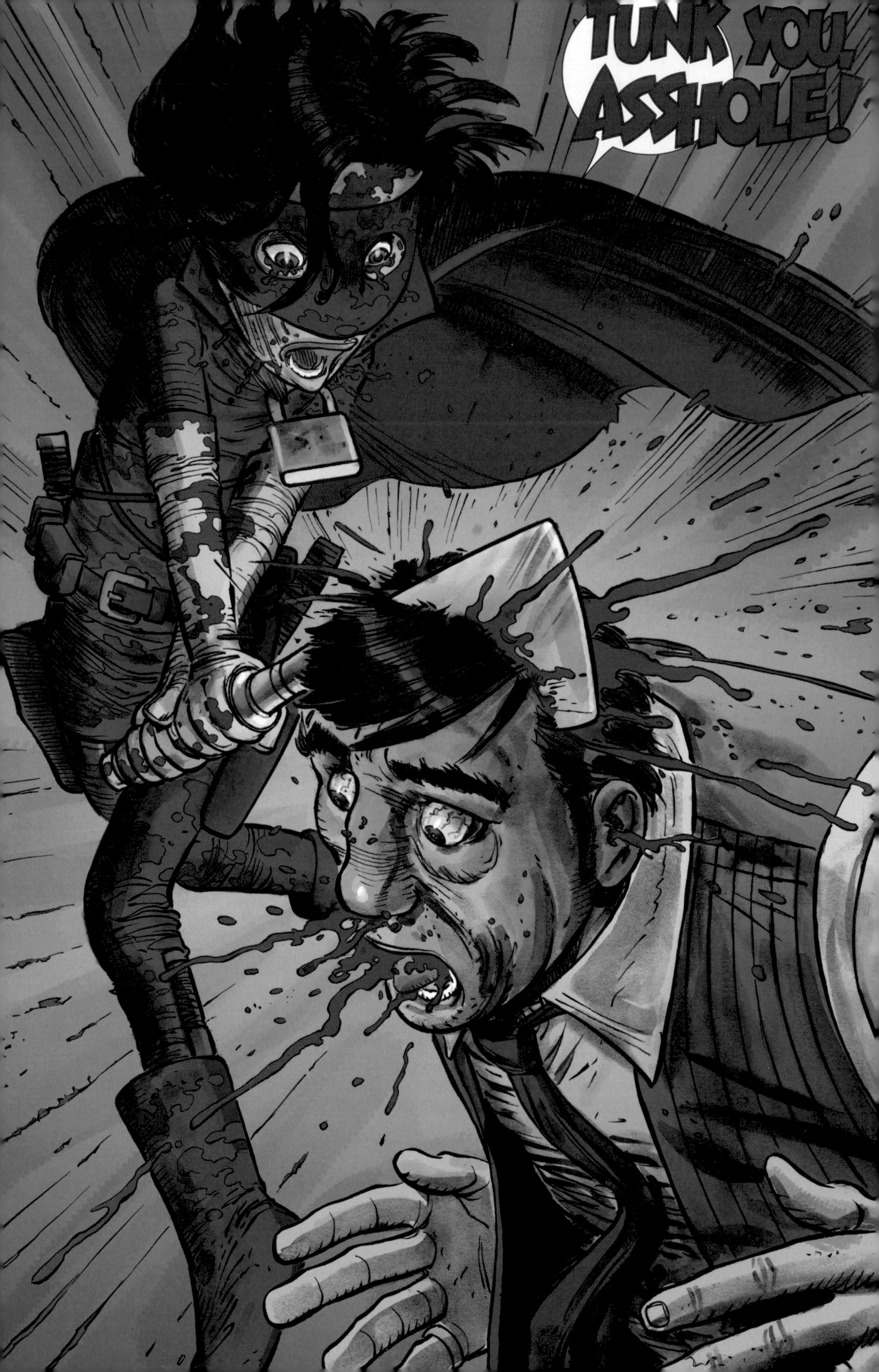
TUNK YOU, ASSHOLE!

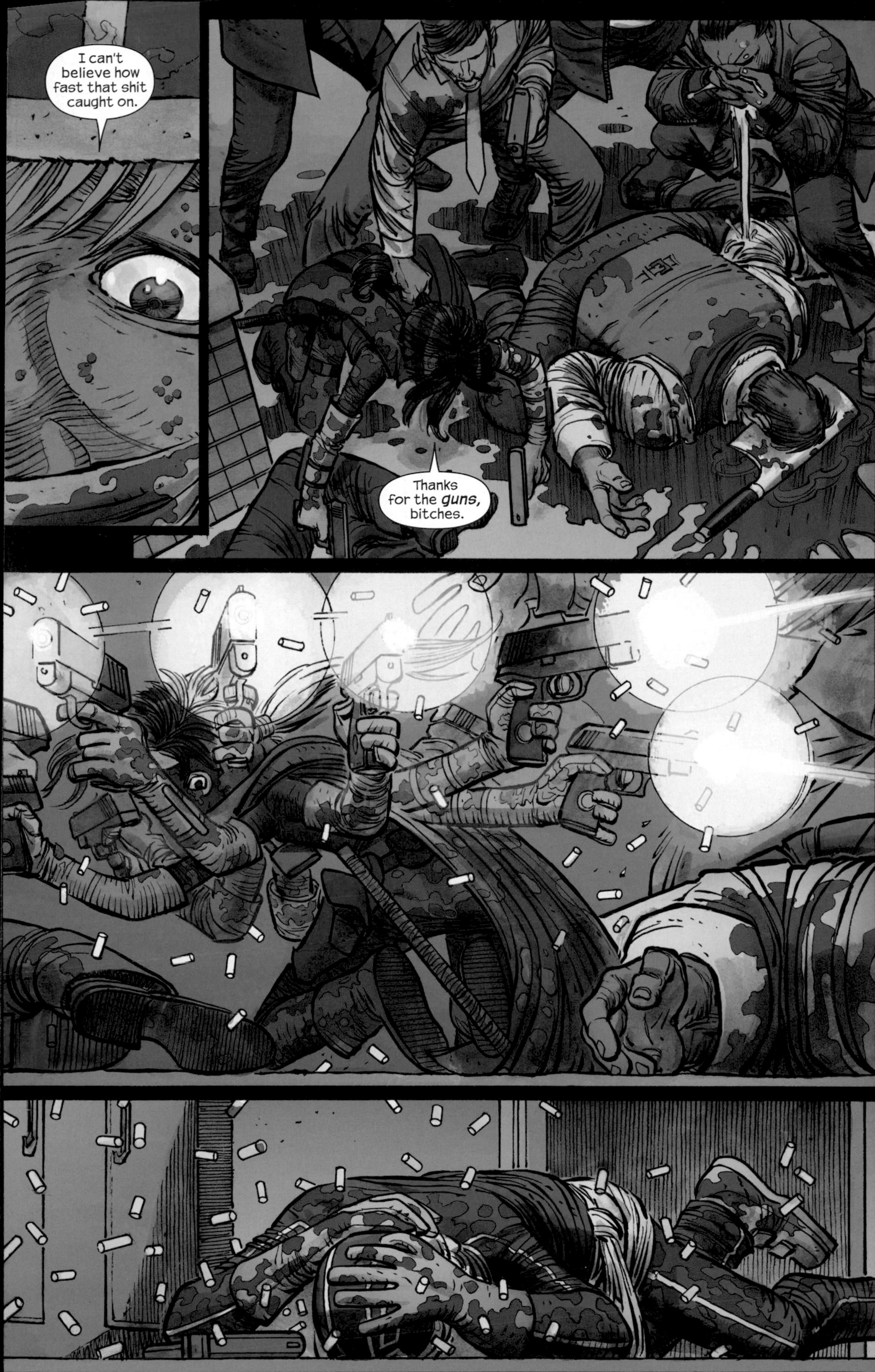
I can't believe how fast that shit caught on.
Thanks for the guns, bitches.

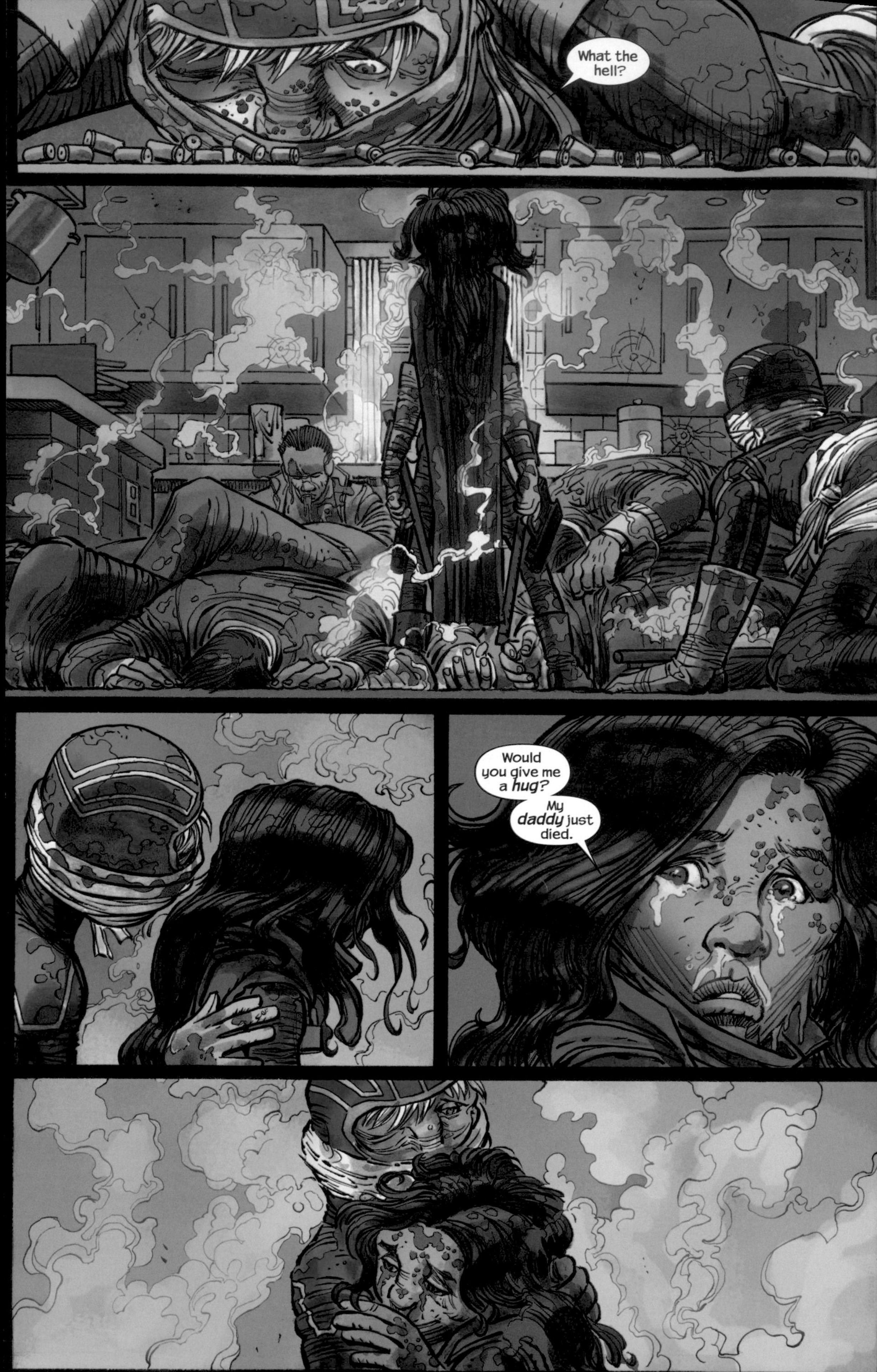
What the hell?
Would you give me a *hug*?
My *daddy* just died.

Thirty-four stiffs were found in that building and, just like every other time Hit-Girl took a life, the whole thing was blamed on *gang-related violence*.

The cops knew *something* was going on, but word online was they actually kinda *liked* it.

Hit-Girl and me became a *legend* on those forums.

We were Batman and Robin. Green Arrow and Speedy. Wonder Woman and that *dykey-looking* chick she used to hang out with in the *forties*.

But Hit-Girl's ambitions died with her father.

She wanted to be *Mindy McCready* for a while and so we tracked down the mom who had never stopped *searching* and gave her back the baby she was missing.

But don't feel too sorry for me. I'd gone from loser to cultural phenomenon in the space of six months.

Superheroes are where I used to hide because real-life was dull, but now life was just as cool as anything happening to *Peter Parker* or *Scott Summers*.

I'd started a trend and all across the country a whole gang of imitators were dressing up and fighting crime because I'd made it *fashionable*.

I'd reshaped the world the way I'd always *wanted* it, and it doesn't get much better than *that*.

Top floor, please!

No problem. Something special goin' on upstairs?

You can read about it in tomorrow's papers.

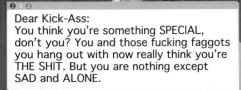

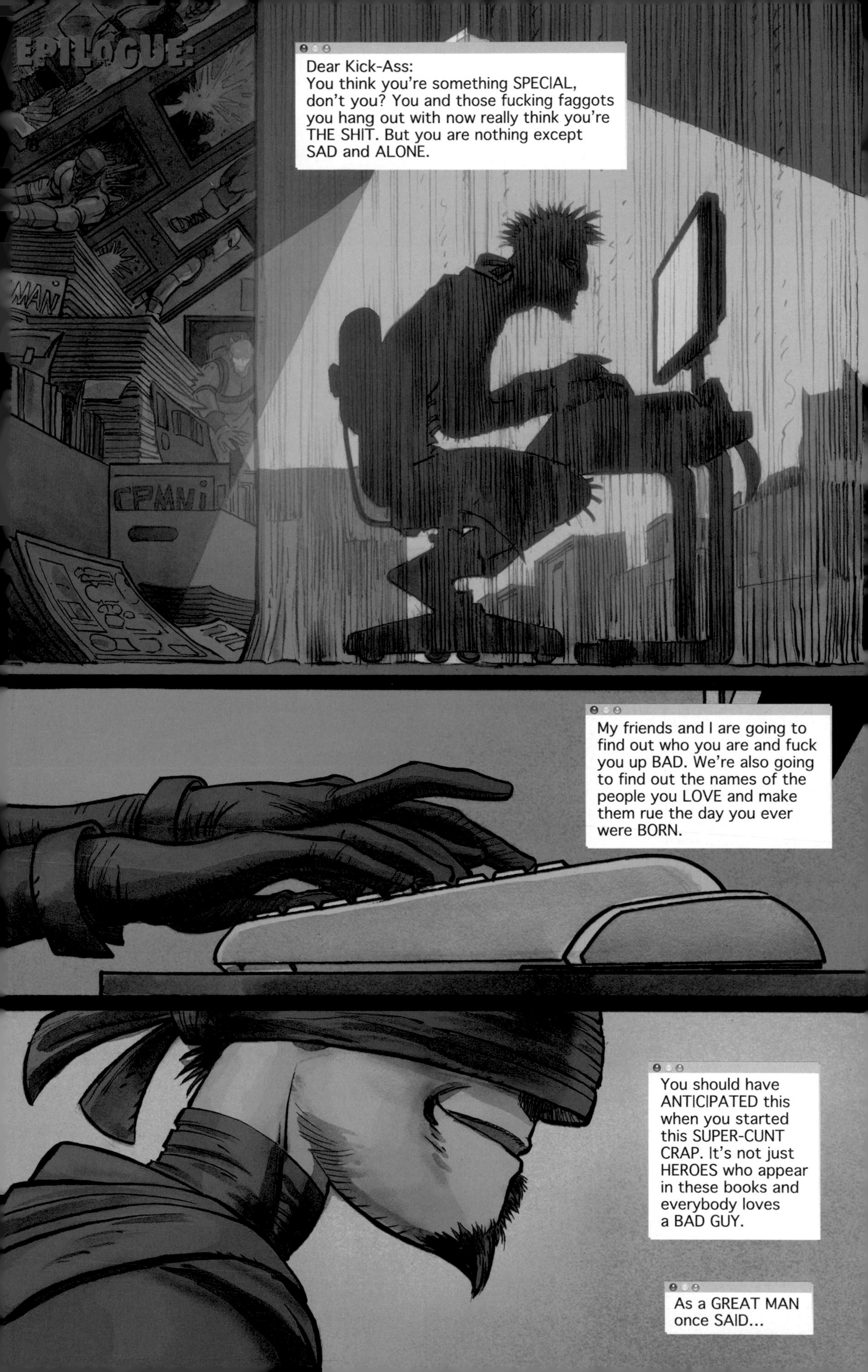

Dear Kick-Ass:
You think you're something SPECIAL, don't you? You and those fucking faggots you hang out with now really think you're THE SHIT. But you are nothing except SAD and ALONE.

My friends and I are going to find out who you are and fuck you up BAD. We're also going to find out the names of the people you LOVE and make them rue the day you ever were BORN.

You should have ANTICIPATED this when you started this SUPER-CUNT CRAP. It's not just HEROES who appear in these books and everybody loves a BAD GUY.

As a GREAT MAN once SAID...

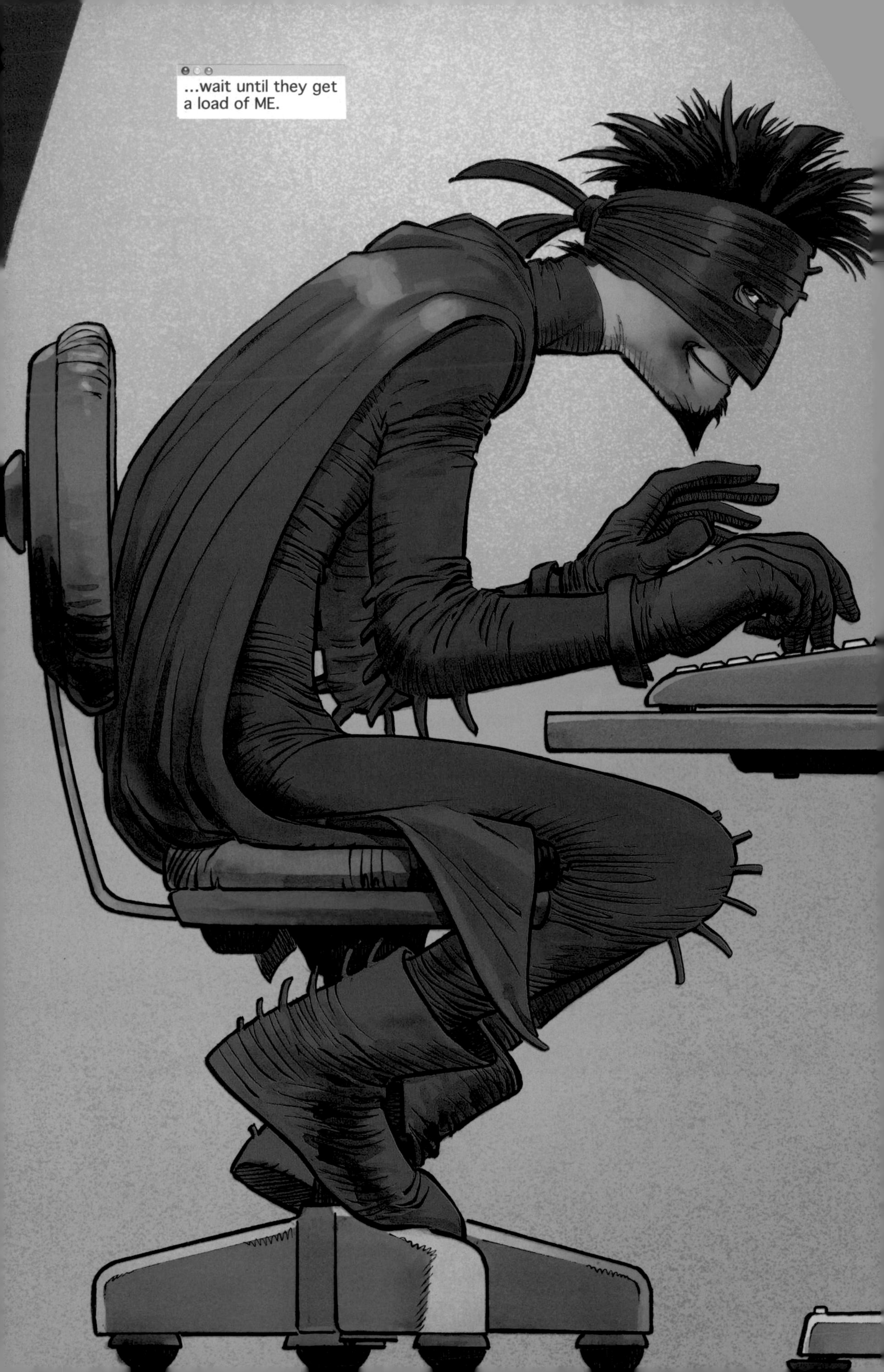
...wait until they get
a load of ME.

END OF BOOK ONE

KICK

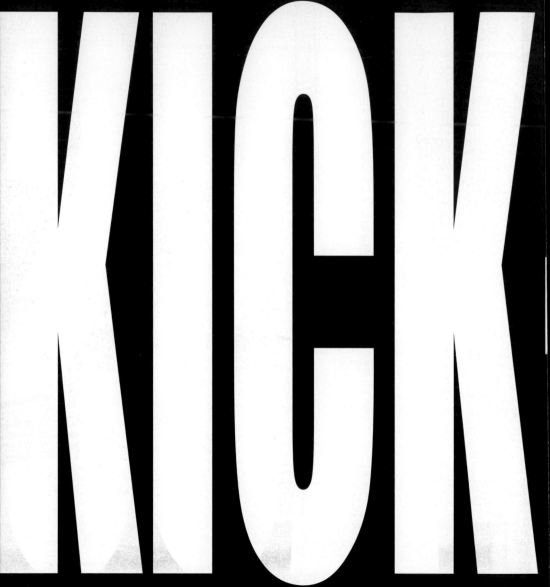

-ASS

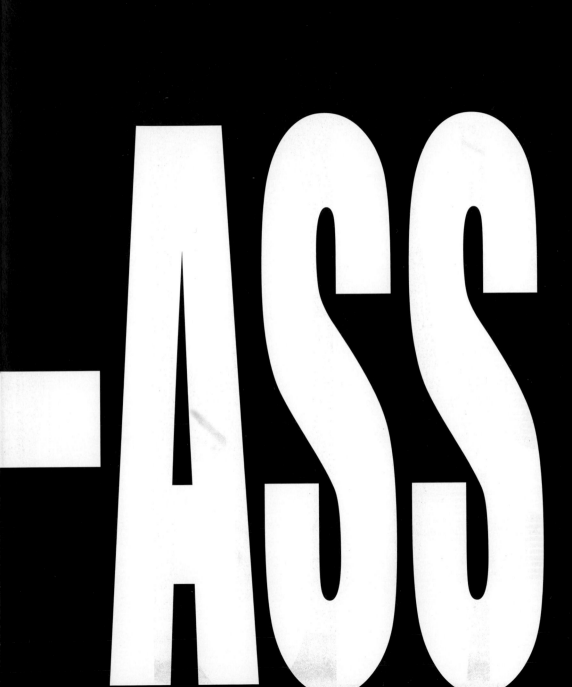

MARK MILLAR has been one of the key writers for Marvel Comics in the 21st century. Millar's first major contribution to Marvel was *Ultimate X-Men*, which achieved great creative and commercial success throughout his two-year run. Working with artist Bryan Hitch on *The Ultimates*, Millar surpassed his own success with that commercial and critical darling. Next, joining up with some of the industry's top creative talent, the Scottish writer took on two of Marvel's most iconic characters: Spider-Man and Wolverine. While working on creator-owned books like *Wanted*, turned into a Hollywood blockbuster staring Angelina Jolie, he penned *Civil War*, the epic miniseries that definitively reshaped the landscape of Marvel's heroes. More recently, Millar has reunited with Hitch on *Fantastic Four* and with *Civil War* artist Steve McNiven in both the pages of *Wolverine* and the upcoming *Nemesis*, as well as returning to the Ultimate Universe with *Ultimate Avengers*.

JOHN ROMITA JR. is a modern-day comic-art legend. A loyal Marvel artist since the late '70s, he has followed in his father's footsteps and helped keep the Romita name on the list of top-shelf talent. Timeless runs on *Iron Man, Uncanny X-Men, Amazing Spider-Man*, and *Daredevil* helped establish him as his own man artistically, and his art on *Wolverine* is arguably the decade's most explosive comic art—trumped perhaps only by his own work on the massive summer blockbuster event *World War Hulk*. JRJR has also paired with renowned writer Neil Gaiman for *The Eternals*, their reworking of the classic Marvel Comics characters, and has recently returned to *Amazing Spider-Man*; he will follow that up with another high-profile Marvel series.

TOM PALMER has worked as an illustrator in the advertising and editorial fields, but he has spent the majority of his career in comic books. His first assignment, fresh out of art school, was on *Doctor Strange*, and he has gone on to lend his inking talents to many of Marvel's top titles, including *X-Men, The Avengers, Tomb of Dracula*, and more recently *Punisher, Hulk*, and *Ghost Rider*. He lives and works in New Jersey.

DEAN WHITE is one of the comic industry's best and most sought-after color artists. Well-known for his work on titles such as *The Amazing Spider-Man, Punisher, Dark Avengers, Captain America, Black Panther, Wolverine* and countless more, Dean's envelope-pushing rendering and color palette bring a sense of urgency and power to every page he touches.

CHRIS ELIOPOULOS is a multiple award-winner for his lettering, having worked on dozens of books during the twenty years he's been in the industry—including Erik Larsen's *Savage Dragon*, for which he hand-lettered the first 100 issues. Along with his success as a letterer, he also publishes his own strip *Misery Loves Sherman*, wrote and illustrated the popular *Franklin Richards: Son of a Genius* one-shots, and writes Marvel's *Lockjaw and the Pet Avengers* series.

MICHAEL HORWITZ's student thesis (a five minute documentary about the private lives of cabbages) was met with resounding indifference by NYU, forcing the Virginia native to realize a career in experimental film wasn't in the cards. With a résumé padded to the extreme (and omitting a regrettable excursion into the world of go-go dancing), Michael somehow fooled Marvel Comics into hiring him, where he now edits such titles as Laurell K. Hamilton's *Anita Blake* and Stephen King's *The Dark Tower*.

JOHN BARBER self-published his own comics before joining the world of webcomics, and later co-wrote a book called *Webcomics*, with Steven Withrow. In 2003, Barber joined the Marvel Comics editorial team and became editor of the Wolverine franchise, before leaving to pursue a freelance career— including a return to comics on the web (webcomicsnation. com/thejohnbarber). He stuck around on *Kick-Ass*, though, which is a hell of a way to go out, editorially speaking.

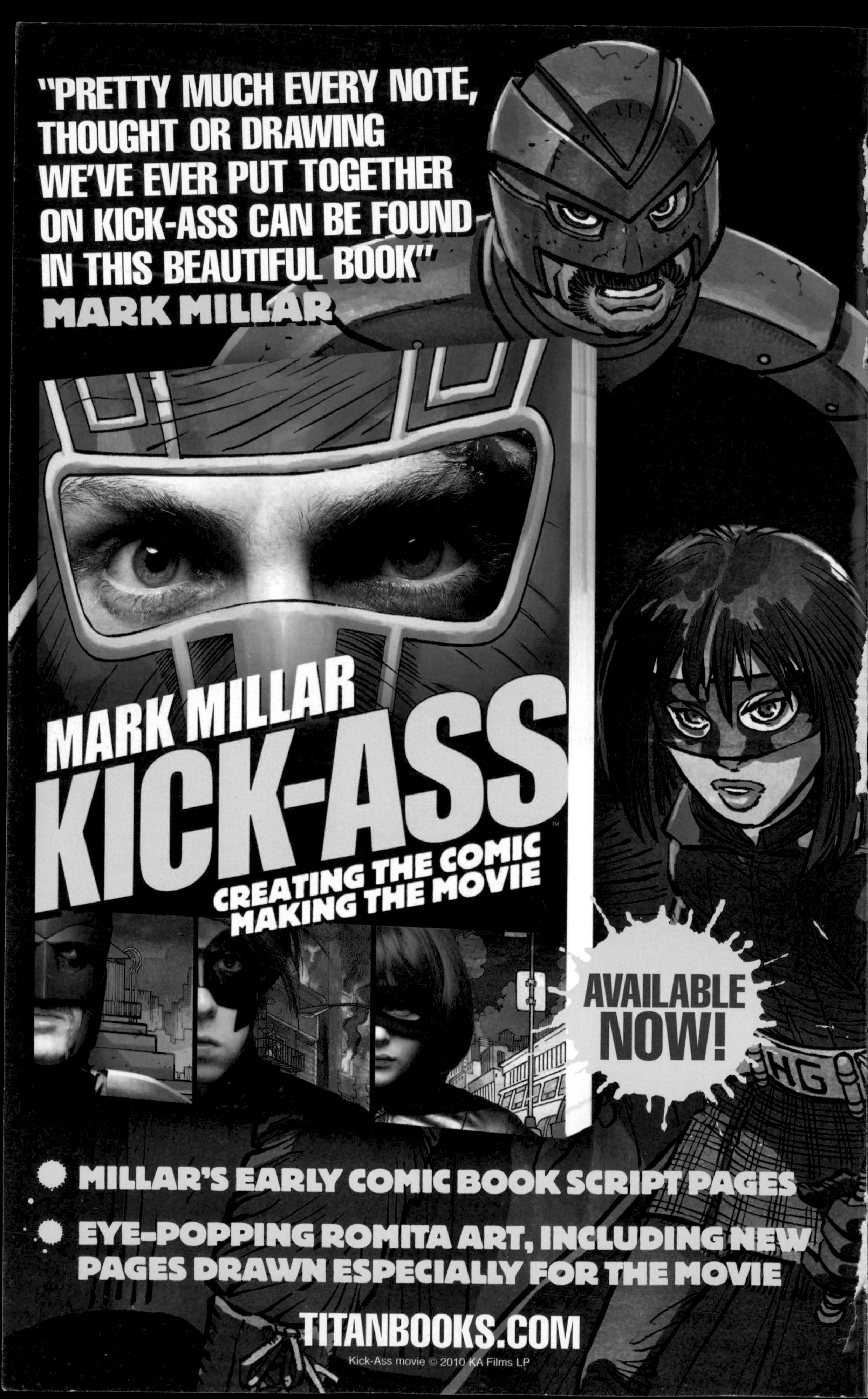

"PRETTY MUCH EVERY NOTE, THOUGHT OR DRAWING WE'VE EVER PUT TOGETHER ON KICK-ASS CAN BE FOUND IN THIS BEAUTIFUL BOOK"
MARK MILLAR
MARK MILLAR
KICK-ASS™
CREATING THE COMIC
MAKING THE MOVIE
AVAILABLE NOW!
HG
• MILLAR'S EARLY COMIC BOOK SCRIPT PAGES
• EYE-POPPING ROMITA ART, INCLUDING NEW PAGES DRAWN ESPECIALLY FOR THE MOVIE
TITANBOOKS.COM
Kick-Ass movie © 2010 KA Films LP